THE
EVOLUTION
OF **HER**

THE
EVOLUTION
OF HER

*Redefining Your Beliefs about
Your Feminine Identity*

Heather Stanislaus

LIFT PUBLICATIONS
New York, New York

Lift Publications
New York, New York
www.evolutionofher.com
info@evolutionofher.com

Library of Congress Control Number: 2015902063

ISBN: 978-0-9864379-0-8 (paperback)
ISBN: 978-0-9864379-1-5 (ebook)

*For all the women of the past
who sacrificed so that we could become.*

"Would you tell me, please, which way I ought to go from here?"

"That depends a good deal on where you want to get to," said the Cat.

"I don't much care where——" said Alice.

"Then it doesn't matter which way you go," said the Cat.

"——so long as I get somewhere," Alice added as an explanation.

"Oh, you're sure to do that," said the Cat, *"if you only walk long enough."*

—Lewis Carroll, *Alice in Wonderland*

CONTENTS

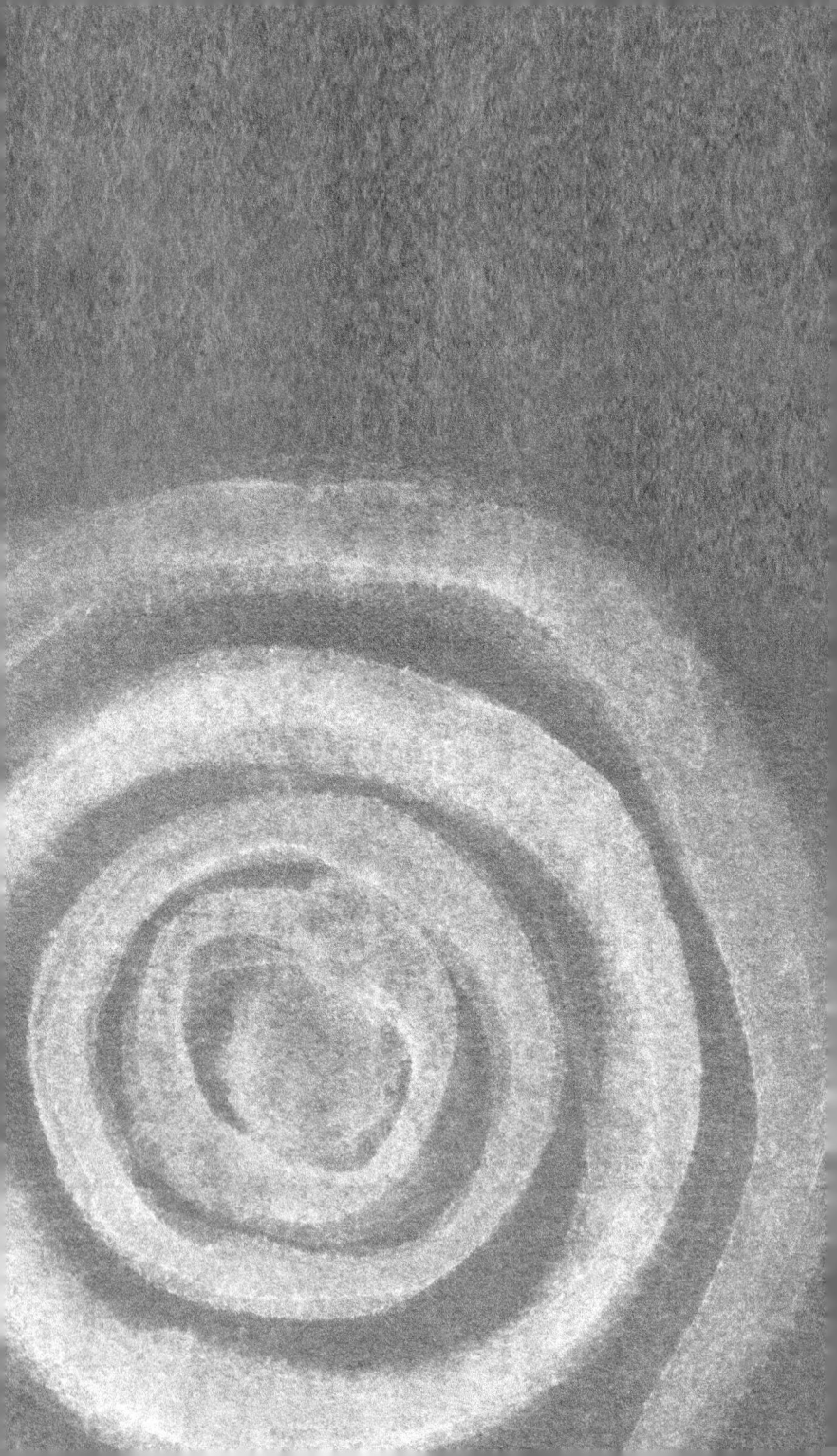

ACKNOWLEDGMENTS

I would like to acknowledge the following people who have helped me to evolve:

Christopheray, for stretching me beyond the confines of my mind and teaching me how to reach my edge without going over it.

Ty, my white rabbit, for showing me new paths of acceptance, truth, and living.

All of my family, friends, and colleagues for your continued support and encouragement along this journey. I am deeply honored.

INTRODUCTION

It is deceptively simple. You are not what you believe.

Our reality is based on our interpretation of what we see, hear, taste, smell, and touch. We witness, and then our intellect interprets, labels, and judges based on our culture, experiences, and education. These interpretations form the basis of our beliefs and perception of our reality.

We have thousands of beliefs relating to almost everything that we can comprehend in the universe, and to much that we can't. Woven together, these beliefs form the basis of our understanding.

Most of our beliefs, especially our deeply held beliefs, aren't truly ours. Rather, they come from the collective belief system of the world. That is, we were never given the opportunity to choose most of our beliefs.

Take the example of religion. Many of us didn't choose our religion. Most religious beliefs are inherited from our families based on the time and place we were born. If you were born in the time of the ancient Greeks, you would be polytheistic; you would believe that different gods govern the sun, the sea, the afterlife, and so forth. If you were born in India, you might be a Hindu and believe in reincarnation. If you were born in China there is a great chance you would be an atheist.

The same holds true for most of our beliefs. They are an accident of birth and culture. Yet, we cling to our beliefs and define ourselves on a set of principles that we never chose.

Just because you believe something doesn't make it true. We think our beliefs are the truth merely because we accept them as the truth. It brings us peace when our beliefs make us feel in harmony with the world. It is problematic when our beliefs cause us pain.

I became interested in this fascinating phenomenon of beliefs when my beliefs about how I should live my life caused me pain. As a young woman, I believed that in order to be happy I had to follow a prescribed life plan of marriage and children. My image of a complete woman didn't align with my reality. I wasn't following the script and, as a result, experienced personal struggles. At times I felt like I was drowning in a sea of expectations barely able to hold my head above water. In an effort to resolve my internal conflict I began to investigate who I was by asking myself a few questions. One of those questions was: *"Why do I believe what I believe?"* More specifically, *"Why do I believe my life has to follow a defined plan?"*

It has long occurred to me that to undermine a person's beliefs is to undermine that person because we confuse who we are with what we believe. We falsely think we are our beliefs. But beliefs aren't who we truly are. They don't exist outside of us; they *only* exist in the microcosm of our minds. They aren't reality. They are simply thoughts.

The mistake we make with self-identifying with our beliefs is the cause of much of our internal conflict and suffering. One of the greatest challenges we face as humans is to critically examine our beliefs. When we see our beliefs as the *only* truth, it creates biases that are self-limiting and prevents us from seeking greater understanding of life. It narrowly locks us into a set of ideals that are inflexible and can easily make us intolerable of those different than ourselves. In order to evolve, we must examine our beliefs. That, of course, takes courage, but is ultimately the price we must pay to get to know our true self.

A deeply held cross-cultural belief is marriage. The practice of marriage has existed in societies past and present. In most cultures it is the shared opinion that when a person comes of age they find a suitable partner, get married, and have children—all in that order. Marriage is a universal cultural belief that is an accepted truth and has become part of our collective consciousness. Those who don't conform to the rules and follow the "path" society has defined are generally considered to be living outside societal norms.

When I began to take a closer look at my understanding of marriage it helped me to understand that my own beliefs didn't have to be so rigid. Although marriage is a universal practice, there is no universal definition of what constitutes marriage. There are multitudes of marital arrangements that have been evolving since the beginning of time. Marriage has meant different things to different people at different times and in different places. If you look up the definition of marriage you will find hundreds of different meanings. If you are an Evangelical Christian, then marriage is defined as the union between a man and a woman. In more liberal faiths, it is defined as the union of two people who love one another. In some countries, such as Kenya and Saudi Arabia, it is legal for men to marry multiple wives. Certain groups of people practice group marriage where multiple men and women become husbands and wives in common.

Marriage is such a widely practiced social convention in our society that there are a staggering number of stigmas associated with it, ranging from stigmas about getting married "too young" or "too old" to having an age discrepancy between you and your partner, the amount of time you have known someone before marrying them, marrying someone of the same gender, marrying someone outside of your race or religion, having been previously married, the number of times you have been married, and more. The list is exhaustive.

One of the greatest social stigmas in our society is that of a person who never marries. And women seem to bear the lion's share of the shame since marriage is viewed as part of the feminine identity.

For a long time, I felt ashamed, confused, and anxious about being single. I was constantly being asked—often to the point of feeling harassed—when I was going to get married. I somehow veered off the "traditional" path and desperately wanted to find my way back so I could feel normal and accepted. However, when marriage didn't happen for me within the timeframe I anticipated it would, I was plagued by self-doubt, unhappiness, and anxiety about my future. I constantly questioned my value because I hadn't attained the social status that everyone, including me, believed I needed in order to be happy. After a while I felt that I must not be worthy of a partner and marriage. The fact that I wasn't married served as my evidence that I wasn't "good enough" —and not "woman enough."

That is the narrative I told myself and accepted as my truth.

My belief was that in order to be happy I had to follow the inherited plan of the feminine identity, which was getting married and having children. My problem, as I saw it, was that if I never got married my life couldn't be complete, that there was no way I could ever be happy. At times, it felt like it wasn't just me who felt this way, but that the world felt so too.

I constantly worried what would happen to me if I didn't get married. Would I have to grow old alone? What would people think of me? What would become of me? I didn't want to be seen as a failure. And so, I began to fear my future and wasn't living in my present. Before I knew it, my fear consumed me and began running my life. I wasn't living life, but trying to achieve a social ideal.

Eventually, I realized that if I wanted to better understand what was causing my suffering, I had to investigate the source of my needs and desires. I had to make friends with my fear and let go of who I thought I was supposed to be. I had to better understand the story of my beliefs.

Doing so allowed me to find the space and freedom to live my life for myself. After much reflection, I realized that my *belief* about who I needed to be was underlying my suffering.

It is often said, you only lose what you cling to. I didn't kill the dream of finding my life partner. Instead, I decided to go straight to the source of my beliefs to eliminate my longing. I freed myself from the need, my attachment to the belief that my life had to be a certain way.

Along my journey, I realized my experience wasn't isolated but shared by countless women. At some point, most women have had to face their beliefs about their feminine identity. We strive to balance the expectations of the feminine identity with the way we want to live our lives. Our shared struggle is the desire to desperately define our own paths and not be beholden to the "conventional" path that gives us few options of who we can be. It is the fight for free will and the freedom to choose and customize the lives we want to live.

There are many social and psychological forces that influence our beliefs and desires. In order to live our best lives, as defined by ourselves, it is essential to understand these forces and how they influence our beliefs. When we are able get underneath the surface of our thinking to explore who we are, something very beautiful emerges. We create the space to be free and live our best lives. Each of us has the power to achieve peace in our lives. We can create renewed energy by appreciating our lives instead of trying to attain an image. We can channel that energy into creating the lives we want, with no apologies and no regrets.

There is no shortage of opinions and advice on how you should be living your life. Each of us has a multitude of people telling us who we should be, how we should act, what we should want, and what we should believe. The purpose of this book isn't to become another one of those voices for you. Rather, this is an open invitation to examine your individual beliefs and the social norms that may be driving you to believe a prescribed life plan is your destined path. It is an opportunity to examine your beliefs about your feminine identity against a backdrop of modernity. I hope to serve as support for you as you navigate your journey of personal empowerment and seek to define your life according to your own values and goals.

I don't speak to you as a relationship expert, self-help guru, or someone who claims to have it all figured out. I speak to you as an individual. As a woman who experiences things as you do. As a woman who is on a journey in search of her personal truth. I can only offer you seeds of thought, which I hope may serve as an impetus for you to begin your personal journey.

—— PART I ——

Dawn

CHAPTER 1
Changing Expectations

The only way to change the expectations of the pre-existing paradigm is if we are the change. It is simply a shift in perspective. We can't wait or expect the world to change it for us; however, we can be more deliberate in our outlook and choices.

THERE HAVE BEEN several defining moments in history for women that have all offered the same hope of liberating women from being defined solely in terms of their sex. They have freed women from oppression. They have provided legal rights of equality. They have opened closed doors. They have given women new meaning. They were all relevant. And they were all necessary.

One of these moments came in 1963 when Betty Friedan published a revolutionary book in which she labeled the problem of gender oppression the "feminine mystique." The publication of her book *The Feminine Mystique* was a cultural shift in women's social history and changed the nation's view on the role of women in America.

The feminine mystique is best described as the beliefs and institutions that misguided Americans to believe that there was no greater destiny for a woman other than to be a housewife and mother. It was based on the belief system that women were incapable of anything more than that, which was underpinned by the educational, social, and political systems of that era.

I remember learning how this book was a major cultural reference for women during its time. I decided it was due time I read it, as it might shed light on the current-day gender expectations of women. Although it had been over 50 years since Friedan's book was written, I soon discovered that it contains the cultural keys to many of our current-day gender issues and what we still define as feminine normalcy. Like then, we are at a defining moment in history where women are in search of a new identity.

Women like you and me are seeking to redefine our lives. We no longer want to be beholden to the narrative of the feminine identity that gives us one path of what defines a woman's life.

It is well known that one of the narratives that pervade our cultural thinking is that a woman's life is incomplete unless she gets married and has children. This ideal is held regardless of gender; however, it is women who feel the onus to fit into this social standard. It is believed that in order to achieve personal fulfillment and any semblance of what is considered feminine normalcy we must follow the same path. If we willfully choose another path, or detour off the path, then we are shamefully stripped of our feminine identities.

It has been five decades since women have shed the cultural

skin of agreement that feminine fulfillment can only be found playing housewife and mother. In these decades, socially dictated gender roles have undergone considerable change. However, socially constructed gender roles still exist, and many young people do still feel the pressure to conform to them.

The belief that a woman's existence is meaningless without marriage and children is an indoctrinated narrative that has been passed down from generation to generation. It isn't coincidental that women feel this way; it is the dream of most little girls. We are innocent in our understanding of this belief because it existed long before us and was imparted to us. As young girls we are taught that we must be "good girls," work hard, fall in love, marry, and have children. This is a cultural axiom.

If we look beyond the narrative that is supposed to underlie our lives, we can see that this belief is a function of our collective consciousness. Our social, cultural, and religious influences propagate this ideal making it part of the collective belief system to the extent that it has become the accepted truth. As children, we usually don't question the system. As adults, it is common for us to question ourselves when we aren't living according to social convention. Any place we deviate challenges our belief system and causes us to suffer.

It has been many years since women achieved "liberation" in the United States—although perfect parity still doesn't exist. Sadly, many women around the world remain the hostages of biased societies. In many parts of the world girls are forced to become child brides, women are denied an education, or endure human right violations, such as female genital mutilation and honor killings. In some places women are forbidden to journey beyond their doorsteps without being covered up or accompanied by a man. For those of us living in more progressive societies, these things are appalling. For that reason, as liberated women we should embrace our real advantages.

For many women, our accepted role has gradually been transformed to take on greater meaning and purpose, landing us in leading roles outside the home in diverse arenas, including politics, business, education, and you name it. An increasing number of women pursue higher education, command executive-level positions, and hold higher office. We are different from any generation that has preceded us. Yet, even given our advancement there still seems to be the expectation for most women to marry and start a family to feel whole. Like many aspects of our lives, change in our beliefs is slow as our societal evolution outpaces our thinking.

I think of my maternal grandmother who was discouraged by her mother from fulfilling her professional dreams of becoming a dentist so she could focus exclusively on fulfilling her personal destiny to be a wife and mother. In an attempt to feel normal, my grandmother conformed, dropping pursuit of any other dreams she had for herself. She became a wife at 20, a first-time mother at 21, and later had 12 more children. She had 13 children not of her own preference, but because women in her era had limited say and no access to birth control. She resigned herself to being a housewife for the rest of her life, dissolving all of her personal dreams and instead following the path that was provided to her. Like so many other women of that time she embraced her role with strength, love, and compassion.

I compare and contrast that with my own thinking almost

a hundred years later. As I attempt to rewind the hands of time and transport myself into my grandmother's shoes to consider how she must have felt about her choices, I suspect that many young women today may feel the same way she did about her feminine identity. We are divided between the desire to live up to the expectation of the feminine identity and the desire to lead happy, successful, and fulfilling lives. We are torn between our desire to establish a career and raise a family. We wonder if we can do both or must make a sacrifice of one to fully realize the potential of the other.

Gradually, I realized that getting married and having babies is a shared dream and a calling for women of all races, religions, and cultures. Although times have changed and we have many more opportunities than our grandmothers ever had, we haven't entirely accepted our new realities when it comes to our personal lives. Many of us cling to old systems and ideologies that don't necessarily reflect our current reality. Often we cling to these beliefs out of fear of not achieving "feminine normalcy."

Regardless of our personal views on feminine fulfillment, the narrative that we must follow the path of marriage and family needs to be acknowledged as it is can interfere with how a woman chooses to live her life. It colors women's decisions on whom and how they date, whom they will choose as a spouse, whether they will pursue certain professional careers, the timing of when they start their families, and if they should stay at home to raise their children.

For some time now women have objected to the age-old belief that the feminine identity is derived through external means. However, as Betty Friedan pointed out in the 1960s, and I point out now: To face the problem is not to solve it.

Complaining is an implicit acceptance of your conditions. The only way to change the expectations of the pre-existing paradigm is if we are the change. It is simply a shift in perspective. We can't wait or expect the world to change itself for us; however, we can be more deliberate in our outlook and choices. That is, we make a conscious change to our beliefs. We relinquish the need to cling to past ideals. We accept needs that old beliefs don't have to have power over us.

Before we can expect the world to change, we must get below the surface, beyond the complaints, and work from the inside out—at the level of meaning and identity. Each of us needs to define for herself a sense of self.

Most conversations on appropriate roles for women just scratch the surface. To evolve, we must change the conversation. We have to, therefore, be the change catalyst. We must examine what fuels the belief that there is a life plan that all women must subscribe to.

Understanding our social and psychological influences help us to understand our ideals and guide us in making personal choices that empower us. Too often we are comfortable blaming others and shifting responsibility for how we feel or what we believe. It is important for each of us to take ownership of our own lives. Understanding what motivates our desires helps us to understand those desires better. Then, instead of feeling that we are failing, we will be able to move forward in a healthy and constructive way.

The question that we need to ask ourselves is: Why do we continue to be bound by limiting beliefs that a woman must follow a prescripted life plan?

A big misstep we can make in attempting to examine this

question is to lose sight of the fact that we are human and have basic needs and desires. As people, we want to connect. We want to procreate. We want to belong. It is a very human thing. We don't have to diminish or deny our desires for partnering and having children in the process of defining self. But we can learn to channel those needs in a way that allows us to be free from the belief systems that we have inherited from past generations.

It is time as a people, and more importantly, as individual women, that we examine our thinking about our roles as women in the framework of our contemporary social realities to determine what is going to work for us. Assessments like this shouldn't be considered an attack on marriage. Marriage is not the enemy. There is absolutely nothing wrong with expressing love within marriage—or outside of marriage. There are so many expressions of love. Love is not constrained to one path. Any beliefs of how love should be shared exist only in our heads.

The real issue, as I have come to understand it, is the inherited systems of thought and beliefs that lead us to think we need to be a certain way, want the same thing, or act a particular way. These don't necessarily make us happy or help us reach our full potential.

To live with real meaning you can start by asking yourself the question: What does personal fulfillment mean to me?

Admittedly, there is a fine thread of a new and intricate pattern of thinking being woven in the minds of women. Today's women have diverse views on the image of a woman. We have grown up in a new era and have renewed purpose. That goes a lot further than following the old life plan given to women. We have opportunities that free us from being bound to the same standards as previous generations.

We are at a cultural turning point. We have come so far. But we can't stop now. The time has come to refresh our beliefs about our feminine identities to determine how they align with the values we ascribe to in our current way of life.

CHAPTER 2
Love

There is nothing wrong with desiring love. There is nothing wrong with wanting to make the journey with someone you love. There is nothing wrong with wanting to feel special and worthy. However, it is important to understand that you are special and worthy enough on your own.

TO LOVE AND be loved is our birthright.

Love is a gift. Love teaches us to be compassionate, to heal, to nurture, to forgive. Thus, love is quintessential for our spiritual evolution. It is nourishment for our souls.

As social beings, we desire love, sex, and companionship. It is natural to want a partner with whom we can share our lives and who will make the journey with us. It is part of the human experience.

As children we are pure manifestations of love. All we know how to do is love. Love is very simple when we are young because it is our natural state. This is often why people give love more freely to children. We aren't afraid to say I love you to children or shower them with hugs and kisses. It is a lot easier for us to express our love to a child because we recognize children are true expressions of love. We were all like this at some point. As adults, however, many of us have become restrained in giving love, more defended. We have come to fear one of the greatest gifts of life: the experience of genuine love.

In order to avoid pain and rejection, we close ourselves off to something that is potentially one of life's greatest joys. We have become conditioned to fear love. And as a result, we have forgotten that in order to receive love, we must open our hearts. Love is meant to be shared. The truth that frightens us is that once we open our hearts to fully experience love we are also at risk of receiving pain.

To some jaded individuals, it is considered a sign of weakness to desire love and a relationship. Women are stigmatized for not marrying and then ridiculed as "desperate" for pursuing relationships. Being on the receiving end of these contradictory judgments can be frustrating. Feeling shame for desiring love is ripe with internal conflict. Mostly, we therefore deny our true desires for love and finding a lifelong mate.

If you want to experience love, then honor that feeling. It is a beautiful thing to share your love with someone special. As humans we are fueled by love. You should never feel bad about desiring something so innate. If you desire love and a relationship, then, by all means, embrace that. Don't allow other people's judgment to influence your feelings or prevent you from pursuing your true desires. Claiming that you desire to share your life with someone special doesn't make you desperate. It doesn't mean that you aren't a happy, fulfilled person. In fact, it makes you very human.

It is fundamental and universal to desire love. Why else would we have been created to feel such a powerful emotion? Although this is true, we can desire love and pursue intimate relationships outside of marriage. If we love someone, then we don't need marriage to experience that love. We can, and should, love regardless of formalizing that bond through marriage. So then, why is marriage considered essential in our society?

How would you feel if you met the love of your life and he adored and wanted to spend the rest of his life with you, but he didn't want to get married? Many of us would end a seemingly perfect relationship if it doesn't fit into the social convention of marriage. How come love isn't enough? Why aren't we satisfied with experiencing the love that surrounds us every day?

The love from our relationships isn't enough because we told ourselves it isn't enough. We believe it isn't enough. Instead of viewing marriage as a complement to the rest of our experiences, it is a central focus of our lives. We have been taught to believe that feelings of loneliness can only be satiated by merging with a partner in marriage. Of course this is a complete denial of the pain and loneliness many of us feel in our troubled marriages.

In many instances, people marry because of their fear-based needs for someone to commit to them so that they don't have to be alone. In *The Road Less Traveled,* M. Scott Peck states, "If we have any purpose in mind when we fall in love it is to terminate our own loneliness and perhaps insure this result through marriage."[1] If you believe that marriage is a cure for loneliness and a precursor to your ultimate happiness, then it stands to reason that you don't believe you can be happy without it. You will be attached to the belief that you need marriage for love. You will believe that love isn't enough.

It is more recently that marriage has come to help us preserve a life of endless love. Historically, people didn't marry for love, but for survival and security. In ancient times, marriage was used as a cooperative arrangement to pool resources, such as land, food, and labor. In the Middle Ages, marriage was used by aristocrats and royals to forge alliances with other nations.[2] Marriage hasn't always been about love. We have just come to believe that marriage is about love and so that is the meaning we ascribe to it.

Marriage has become a status symbol. It has come to represent the symbol of a woman's self-worth, in some ways no different than any other object like a handbag, a car, or a big, fancy house. Just like any other symbol, it isn't the object that makes us happy, but the meaning we ascribe to it. Possessing a symbolic object gives us a false sense of security or importance. If I purchase an expensive handbag, for example, it makes me feel good about myself to know I can afford it. It becomes a symbolic representation of who I am. That reassures me. I may even criticize another woman who has an "inferior" bag than mine to make myself feel better. With symbols of status, it isn't only important to obtain them, it is equally important for the rest of the world to recognize and affirm the status of the object. It therefore is an external measure of a person's value and manipulates our self-worth to be directed outwardly.

Because American culture is extremely consumption oriented, we are conditioned to believe that attaining status is life's sole objective. We cling to our status to define who we are. Materialism hinges on the belief that the more you have the more you are. The more boxes you can check off, the better you believe you will be perceived and therefore the better you will feel about yourself—as long as your preconceptions aren't challenged and overridden.

It isn't surprising that marriage is considered a symbol of status for women. For years marriage was the only vehicle that provided women with status. Women weren't allowed to own property, vote, or earn a living. Women obtained their power indirectly through the men they married. Because women were denied basic rights, marriage was a woman's connection to get ahead and obtain access to privilege. A husband's status directly influenced his wife, either elevating or reducing her stature. This is why it is just as important to women to be attached to a partner who has attained a certain level of status himself, whether its money, career, achievements, or education.

How many of us have dreamed of meeting a man who is famous, wealthy, or in a position of power? A man's suitability to be a father certainly factors into a woman's decision of which man will become her mate. Instinctively we want to partner with a suitable man to father our children to ensure our children's futures. If a man is stable or affluent, then chances are, our children will be better off.

But a man with status also helps elevate the status we already seek through marriage. It sometimes gives us as much a sense of self and security, if not more, than our own careers and efforts do. Men don't necessarily use the same measure when choosing a partner. They care less about a woman's status and more about whether she will be a good wife and mother.

For many women, the desire for marriage and love supercedes our self-acceptance. Our self-worth is linked to the attainment of a relationship. We believe if someone else can love and accept us it means we are good enough to love and accept ourselves. The feeling of not being good enough is a sentiment that many women who don't achieve this ideal feel. Whether or not we like to admit it, for many it is true.

We have been taught to believe that we aren't enough without the love of someone else. We have been socially conditioned to believe that marriage is the cornerstone of the feminine identity. This belief existed before us and may very well exist long after we are gone. As little girls we are told fairy tales in which princesses are rescued by their princes, and we imagine ourselves growing up to stand in their shoes. These beliefs are engrained in our religions and social traditions, and hammered into us by our media and institutions. They are embedded in our earliest memories and permanently etched into our thoughts. For little girls, although some of these images are being supplanted by images of new role models who are more powerful and self-defined, the old romantic ideals continues to exist in parallel.

If these beliefs are true, then marriage is self-serving. Many of us exploit marriage to validate our existence.

There is nothing wrong with desiring love. There is nothing wrong with wanting to make the journey with someone you love. There is nothing wrong with wanting to feel special and worthy. However, it is important to understand that you are special and worthy enough on your own. When you are able to appreciate your worth you no longer require anything external to you to accept yourself as you are.

We have been empowered like never before to take action and change our way of thinking. That doesn't mean we give up our dream for partnering and family—if we so chose. Needless to say, there is a distinction between indifference and detachment. We can have an intention without being attached to an outcome.

We can be childlike again and open our hearts to receive the gift of love. We can desire love from a new place of worthiness. This kind of love can bring us a level of satisfaction in our relationships far greater than we could ever imagine. No longer is there a self-seeking need or wanting from our relationships. In this state, we realize it is better for our evolution to have loved than to be loved.

We all have a strong need to defend, preserve, and prove our importance. Most of us are constantly waging a war within ourselves over whether or not we are enough. We struggle to reconcile our desire to feel special and worthy with the image of who we think we should be. There is great shame in believing that you aren't enough. We may not even realize it, but every day we feed ourselves lies about why we aren't good enough. Well, who aren't we good enough for? If we aren't enough to please everyone else from our parents and family, to our teachers, friends, or significant others, does it really matter? It should matter more that we please ourselves.

We don't believe we are enough because of the false ideals of perfection that we are fighting to achieve. We are trying to be the person that exists in our beliefs. To be the person that everyone expects us to be. We suffer because we struggle to conform to images instead of being our true self. All the mixed messages and competing personas of who we should be lead us to look to others for validation. As a result, we are constantly seeking acceptance.

We spend countless hours seeking acceptance and affirmation from others. We spend a considerable amount of time learning the expectations of others and conforming to the image of who we should be. Significantly more time than we ever spend getting to know ourselves.

What makes you unsatisfied with your life? What is it you wish you had that would make you happy? What are you envious of? What do you wish to change about your physical appearance? Do you experience a constant internal conflict about whether you are enough? If you believe that you aren't enough and can't accept yourself, you are more likely to turn toward others to help you feel better about yourself.

Part of our evolutionary growth is understanding the energies that drive our desires. Often our desires are disguised as something completely different. For instance, take a person who is driven to make money. On the surface she is focused on making tons of money, but what she truly desires is the power to control her life. Or take a person who desperately desires fame. Deep down her desire for fame is the need to have a purpose.

The only way to uncover our true desires is to go beyond the desire to the origination within our thinking. This is true about any desire, not just the desire for love or a relationship.

If you want to understand yourself better, you must dig deep and ask yourself questions, continuously pushing beyond the boundaries of your comfort zone, and perhaps even daring to go down paths that are unfamiliar to you. Understanding is the key. When you are grounded in understanding, then you can achieve personal freedom.

───── **PART II** ─────

*Social and Cultural
Influences*

CHAPTER 3
The Evolution of Her

*We can adopt a fresh perspective for what best works for us
in our contemporary times. Such is true for anything in life.
We shouldn't base our desires and decisions on how things
were. Rather, we should base them on how things are and
how we would like them to be.*

IN NATURE THERE is a fundamental law: adapt or die.

Change is the very essence of life. Every living organism
must be able to adapt to the changing conditions in its environment or else face extinction. Although this concept is one of
the many laws of the natural world, the same isn't true of our
thinking. It often takes years for cultural beliefs to keep pace
with our evolution. While individuals often have the capacity to
change their personal thinking, change in our group thinking is
slow. There is often a cultural lag in our ideals while new agree-
ments are being reached.

As an example, in many households today where women
work full time, just like their husbands, it is still the expectation that they are responsible for the household chores. When

women were full-time housewives, it was understood that their primary role was to manage the home. Nowadays, with the shift of women into the workforce this is more of an unreasonable expectation. But how often do we hear people defend that this is a woman's role because that's how its always been done. If we understand the cultural context in which these gender roles originated then expectations should adjust to better reflect the new realities of working women. But in all these years, many haven't. That is because group thinking hasn't yet caught up with our social evolution.

Despite the new roles that women have assumed and all the dreams women now pursue without apology, our desire to adopt the life plan of marriage and children hasn't changed much since preceding generations. Not only is it the expectation that one must get married, there is also still the expectation that it needs to happen within a designated timeframe. How many of us compare the age we marry and have children to our mothers and grandmothers? It is unfair to compare who we are and how we live today with our foremothers some 50 to 100 years ago. They lived in different times that drove them to make the best decisions for their lives in the cultural framework of their time.

We are different from those who preceded us. Today's women have a different mindset given our social influences, such as higher education, more equality, and greater opportunity. We can adopt a fresh perspective for what best works for us in our contemporary times. Such is true for anything in life. We shouldn't base our desires and decisions on how things were. Rather, we should base them on how things are and how we would like them to be.

Much of our thinking about our feminine identity is tied to the inherited cultural norms about what it is to be a woman. In a time when a woman can define for herself who she will be, we continue to be bound by old images of femininity.

We are at an opportune crossroads to break free from these indoctrinations to move forward in a healthy and fulfilling manner. And we must do so.

But before we can proceed we must understand how our social evolution impacts our current beliefs.

Reflecting on the lives and roles of the women of the past, it occurred to me that a pattern of thinking has unknowingly been passed down through the generations that still affect the women of today.

It wasn't long ago that women demanded liberties, such as the right to own property, open bank accounts in their own names, vote, earn a living, obtain an education, and control their reproductive rights. These rights unchained us from being defined exclusively in accordance with our sex.

For a long time women were thought of as inferior, incapable of higher thought and therefore lacking value. Women derived their identities from being wives and mothers because they were viewed as lacking the ability to do anything other than cook, clean, raise children, and serve as sexual objects for the men in their lives. Even when women were granted more equality, it remained a common belief that a woman wasn't a real woman unless she was a wife and mother.

It took years to change the laws and force anti-discrimination legislation through the ranks of government to ensure equality. Although in the United States we now have equal protections under the law, there are still disparities in the wages women earn for comparable work, and women still work a "second shift" at home.

It is mistakenly assumed that women's oppression dates back to the beginning of time. However, it isn't true. If we scroll back in time we see that the first hunter-gather civilizations were egalitarian. Everyone played a role and was respected and valued as contributing to society. Civilizations were smaller tribal communities and no one could survive on their own. As such, there was a co-dependency for survival.[1] Because of a woman's exclusive ability to bear children and nourish infants from her breasts, women performed duties closer to the home.

What later occurred was mutually exclusive gender roles. As civilizations developed and people became less dependent on communal living and more centered on individual family life the need for power and wealth arose. In a fight for control and affluence, women became oppressed due to the vulnerability of birthing and nurturing our infantile offspring.

Because a woman was perceived as inferior, her opportunities for advancement, including educational opportunities, were limited. The denial of intellectual stimulation dwarfed the mental growth and development of women. As a direct result, women lacked financial autonomy. There were little to no opportunities for a woman to be financially independent unless she inherited money from her family. A woman historically needed marriage, and at a much younger age, for financial security.

Women were economically dependent on men for survival and therefore weren't autonomous. The lack of autonomy played a huge factor in the cultural norm of pair bonding. A woman's well-being, affluence, and livelihood were derived through the institution of marriage. A woman's survival was literally tied to that of her husband.

It has long been believed that marriage is part of the feminine identity because it was the cornerstone of a woman's survival and security. That fear-based thinking has unknowingly been passed down from generation to generation. Many of us still carry the fears of the past about needing marriage for our well-being. This is no different than the understanding that has been passed down to men that as a result of their opportunities they don't need to worry about being married. This is evidenced by the clear distinction between a woman's and a man's outlook on marriage. On one hand, women typically dream of the day they get married. Sometimes, they don't even have to marry the right person as long as they aren't the last woman they know to get a ring. On the other hand, many men view marriage as a possibility should the right person come along. The difference in views is unconsciously driven by the fears that have been embedded in our thinking.

Men also worry about financial ruin and survival, but most men don't look to marriage as their primary mechanism to solve the dilemma of sustaining their livelihood. Men have historically been afforded the opportunities of education and advancement. As such, their desire to be married hasn't been grounded in fear. They choose to marry when it best suits them, and as a result, govern their choices.

The subconscious fear that our existence isn't within our control is also a contributing factor to why women's self-worth has long been linked to our beauty and sexuality. It is because, for years on end, women's value was reduced to a physiological level. Women were considered less than whole, stripped of any identity and defined only in sexual terms. We bartered our beauty and feminine abilities in exchange for men's protection out of the sheer desire to survive. Our identities were linked with beauty and sexuality because it was thought of as the only thing we had. That is why men's desire for us makes us feel more powerful.

Women sought respect through the only means that they knew was available: their sexuality. It was our sexuality and beauty that was used to compete for men, and thus ensure our survival. If all you had to look forward to was being a pretty wife, then you had nothing else to fall back on other than your looks. Beauty, sexuality, and fertility were women's bargaining chips, becoming part of the feminine identity and giving them very few alternatives.

In the past, men had the power to control. Women were forced into an inferior role because they were denied the opportunity to be anything greater than that, and for no other reason. But that is changing. Since then, social, political, and technological advancements have leveled the playing field. The emphasis is now one of a knowledge economy. We no longer compete based on our physical strength, but our intellectual capital. Able-bodied men are no longer the only ones who can chop down trees, fight in wars, or be the breadwinners.

There are fewer barriers limiting us. Although inequality still exists, the gap is quickly shrinking. The number of women seeking higher education is increasing. The rising percentage of women in the workforce and in positions of power is continuing to reframe our society to be more equitable. The number of women who are leaders in business and government is on the rise. Unless you are a woman living in poverty or have many children and receive limited support from family and community, you no longer need to be in a relationship for survival.

Marriage is often still thought of in terms of survival. However, most of us living in developed societies no longer need a husband solely for financial support and survival. We may desire to partner, but now with renewed purpose. We can choose to partner from a place of genuine love and not from a place of dependent fear or need. This leads us to experience more fulfilling relationships, which we ultimately desire.

We are living in a time where we can make a new agreement to partner to share our love. Now that we have careers, money, and property, and can even raise children on our own, connecting with a partner can be all about our desire to share our lives, rather than to prove anything, or for the fear we can't survive alone. We must understand, and then let go of, the fears we have adopted from the past that tells us we are worthless on our own. We can simply aim to be happy and incorporate marriage into our lives as one of the elements that contributes to our overall happiness.

We have the opportunity, like never before, to create a life plan based on individuality. Even modern science affords a woman the ability to prolong her reproductive years by storing her eggs for future implantation in her own womb or the womb of a surrogate—albeit her fertility doesn't last indefinitely. However, our thinking hasn't yet caught up with our evolution. Many of us still long for the lives of our foremothers and fantasize about being taken care of. We still fear the possibility of never getting married.

It would be fair to say that considering women's pursuit of financial independence, career advancement, and contributing on a larger scale to society we need to reshape our thinking and expectations. That isn't to say that one can't strive for career, marriage, *and* family. Rather, we can change our expectations and beliefs of the feminine identity in a way that incorporates a modern woman's lifestyle. Would it be fair to say that a woman is free to marry at 35 instead of 25 because she now has the freedom to find out who she really is and what she really wants out of life? Would it be fair to say that the new-age woman remains single without it being considered a tragedy?

It is time to align our thinking to be more representative of our current social conditions.

Relinquish the belief of what history defines as the feminine identity. In order to evolve you must be adaptive to our changing world. Evolve your thinking to define your identity based on your own terms. What does it mean to be you? What works best in your life? How do you achieve personal fulfillment?

THE NOTION OF gender equality is a paradox. We realize that we are equal and capable of achieving our dreams. Yet, as we achieve success, wealth, and personal growth we have more to prove causing a backlash against the idea that we can have it all. It is a false expectation that a woman can successfully balance a career, have a healthy relationship, and raise kids all within a compressed timeframe. It isn't all that common after all.

Women have a growing number of boxes to check off on the "happiness list." We have to constantly prove that we can juggle our newfound seat in society and still be a good wife and mother. Working mothers in particular feel as if they run the risk of people thinking that they aren't capable of doing their jobs and tending their children.

There are so many expectations placed on women to be perfect. The dissonance of messages received from all the voices telling us who we ought to be is deafening.

We no longer need to hold ourselves to these expectations. A woman is supposed to be Superwoman and have a flourishing career, be smart, beautiful, skinny, a good cook, a great wife, a great mother. We think all of these things make us more powerful. But it is the attachment to these ideals that cause us to be powerless. We can easily become consumed with attaining false ideals of perfection. In doing so, we lose control of who we are. We are told we are a "winner" in life if we are able to fit the image of this perfected feminine identity. As a result, we have become busier chasing the dream and imprisoned by the belief that we need to "have it all."

We should be less hard on ourselves.

Anytime you feel an expectation to be something you aren't, realize it isn't your own energy. Your soul has no expectations on you. Expectations by definition aren't what are living inside of you. It is you trying to match your energy to somebody else's energy. That is when you feel the most compromised. Get rid of all of the "expectations" of who you need to be and instead figure out what you want and what makes you happy. When you do, you will feel more fulfilled and your life will be more meaningful.

If your goal in life is to marry, have a family, and pursue other dreams and aspirations, then you are leading a more independent lifestyle than the women of the previous generations.

That is true for most of us. If so, then our thinking should change. But for many of us it hasn't. We still carry the beliefs of past generations even though we live in very different times.

This isn't to diminish the importance that women have historically and currently play in our society as wives and mothers. But only to suggest that we have a greater appreciation for our changing world and, to the extent necessary, alter our thinking to fit the context of our current times.

Evolve your thinking. Everything in life changes, including you. Regardless of your desire to change or not, you will change. How you will evolve is entirely up to you. Set your intention to evolve. Don't get stuck thinking that you or your life needs to be a certain way. Be open to the idea that you are a being who was put here to evolve so that you can learn about yourself and reach your full potential.

Marriage and motherhood can still be a goal, but free from all of the fears of the past. Once we let go of inherited past ideals, we can move forward and define a new future for ourselves, whatever that may look like. That can still entail marriage, but gives us the personal freedom to define that based on our own personal journeys. We can do this by understanding the story of our beliefs. Then, and only then, do we have the power and insight to shift our perspective.

You may decide that you aren't interested in a traditional marriage, but some alternative arrangement that doesn't include legal formalities. You may feel comfortable never marrying. You may choose to wait until you are older to start your family. Or decide that you don't want to be a mother. The choice is yours. Whatever you choose, don't relegate yourself to outmoded beliefs. We live in a changing world and should change along with it.

Like the rest of the natural world, we must adapt or else face the risk of not truly living. When you free yourself from the attachment to the narrative of the old feminine identity, you free yourself from its expectations. And from that comes freedom to discover who you are and who you want to be; to be the true you; to live a holistically fulfilling life; to live your best life according to you.

CHAPTER 4
Rituals & Traditions

We must make personalized decisions based on our current circumstances and what works best for us at the given time, no matter what. We aren't being served by all things at all times. If something is not serving you, then let it go.

WE ARE A ritualistic people. Rituals are an important part of our lives. They are handed down to us and become part of our cultural norms and diverse customs, better known as traditions. Our rituals and traditions play a large role in shaping our belief systems, and through their indoctrination shape our lives and identities.

Every society is ritualistic. This is never truer than in our marriage customs. Like most traditions, marriage is rife with rituals and tradition that are symbolic of our commitment.

In Jewish tradition, the bride and groom are married by a rabbi under a *huppah* and sign the marriage contract, called a *ketubah*. The ceremony is concluded by the groom breaking a glass with his right foot.

An American Christian wedding ceremony traditionally is

performed at the altar of a church. The bride wears a white dress along with something old, something new, something borrowed, and something blue. The couple exchanges rings, which are placed on the ring finger of the left hand.

In a Hindu marriage held in India, a bride wears a colorful *sari* or *lehenga* with henna designs painted on her hands and feet. Absolutely no one wears white to the wedding, not even the bride, as white is considered a color of mourning. The couple get married by a *pandit* (priest) on a *mandap* (temporary wedding altar) with a fire burning between them. Even these customs may vary depending on what region of the country your family is from.

Rituals and traditions are culturally determined based on the time and place we are born. Take the aforementioned wedding traditions. Or take the example of birthday rituals. The simple act of turning a year older is filled with rituals that vary by cultural tradition. In the United States, on someone's birthday family and friends gather. They bring presents, top a cake with flaming candles that correspond in number to the age of the birthday "boy" or "girl," and sing "Happy Birthday." The birthday celebrant makes a wish and then blows out the candles.

By contrast, in Vietnam, everybody's birthday is collectively celebrated on New Year's Day. Children are congratulated on becoming a year older and receive red envelopes that contain cash, or "lucky money."

Despite the cultural differences, our rituals share the same meaning. Regardless of the nature of our rituals, their symbolism helps us interpret our life experiences. They are symbolic celebrations of life. They help unite us in good times and in bad. Think about how joyous it is when we celebrate a friend's birthday, or how touching it is to commemorate our loved ones' lives after they have passed, or how connected we feel on Thanksgiving sitting around the table with our families carving the turkey and giving thanks. These are very endearing and meaningful moments that help us celebrate our experience of life.

If you take a closer look you will see the story of our cultures is revealed through our rituals. They are a reflection of who we are, what we value, and our need to feel connected. They are our social laws, shaping our beliefs about what is normal, acceptable behavior.

Have you ever considered just how ritualistic we really are? We tend to mistake rituals as some sacred or ancient tribal rite. But rituals aren't exclusively sacred or religious practices. Our everyday lives are peppered with rituals, which are performed through the use of objects, gestures, phrases, and actions, ranging from how we greet one another to the time we eat our meals. We swear an oath of allegiance to our nation and to tell the truth in court. In certain cultures, if someone pisses us off, we perform gestures like giving them the middle finger. We cover our mouths when we yawn. We light fireworks to celebrate holidays. We give gifts of flowers and candy on Valentine's Day. We feast on Thanksgiving. We sing on people's birthdays. We perform burial rites.

I never realized how instinctively and unquestioningly we perform rituals until recently. The simple act of saying "God bless you" after someone sneezes, for example, is a ritual we don't question and most don't know the origins. We say it to be kind to one another. In response, the person who sneezed says thank you because it makes them feel cared about. Historians tell us that saying "God bless you" was popularized by Pope Gregory the Great in the Middle Ages. During that time, the Roman population was devastated by a plague that was believed to have been caused by contamination in the air. As such, the Pope prescribed a special prayer for those who sneezed, to ward off the evil.[1]

When we stop to evaluate our rituals and traditions we find many of them belong to a time and place that is no longer relevant. And a good many of them have no significance other than the fact that we are told they are important.

As an example, in most cultures it is customary that a man ask a woman's parents for her hand in marriage. This tradition derives from the era when marriage was considered an exchange of property more than an act of love. Yet today, even if a woman is well into her adulthood, financially independent and mature enough to make a decision as to whom she wants to marry, it is still customary for the man to get her parents' permission. Is it still relevant to ask a woman's parents' permission as if she weren't capable of making that decision on her own?

Contrast this with a custom that arose more recently, which is the gift giving of a diamond engagement ring. Currently, it is customary for a man proposing marriage to get down on bended knee and present his beloved with a diamond ring. Prior to 1930, it wasn't the norm for a woman to receive a diamond ring. The diamond engagement ring became embedded in popular culture from a marketing campaign created by a diamond cartel in the 1930s, after the Great Depression, in an effort to raise falling profits. This was further popularized by an advertising firm that created the slogan "A Diamond Is Forever," forever minting the diamond ring as the ultimate expression of our love.² Today, the ring is considered a symbol of your partner's status, love, and affection for you. If you don't get a diamond engagement ring, or perhaps the ring isn't "big enough," then people may think you are less adored by your partner. Ring giving has become a "tradition" that we cling to that has no value other than the power of sentiment.

Once I realized how ritualistic we are as people I started to pay closer attention to all the rituals I performed unconsciously. I started to become more conscious of my behaviors and thoughts. What I discovered is that although rituals and traditions help to unite us, to a large extent, we use them to conform to socially acceptable norms.

We have a strong need to connect and belong. It is a very human thing to want to be a part of something bigger than us. Our rituals and traditions help us connect and form a kinship with others. They are a shared set of beliefs and practices that unite us with members of our community, like a network or support system.

If you think about it, this is similar to how we form friendships. Generally, we are attracted to our friends because we have something in common with them, like growing up in the same neighborhood, going to the same school, holding similar religious beliefs, doing a similar job, sharing the same hobby, experiencing a similar challenge, or being passionate about the same cause. Commonality connects us. The same is true for rituals and traditions. Sharing rituals and traditions helps bond us to our families, friends, and those who are similar to us. It helps us to feel connected to the larger world.

In the *Anatomy of the Spirit*, Caroline Myss states, "As tribal beings, we are energetically designed to live together, to create together, to learn together, to be together, to need one another.... No one begins life as a conscious "individual" with conscious willpower. That identity comes later and develops in stages from childhood through adulthood. Beginning life as part of a tribe, we become connected to our tribal consciousness and collective willpower by absorbing its strengths and weaknesses, beliefs, superstitions and fears."[3]

Because of our need to belong we are in constant need of acceptance. We rather conform for fear of being rejected. Conformity falsely gives us a sense of satisfaction about how we are living our lives. It is mostly a diversion from taking personal responsibility for our own thoughts and actions. For example, for a long time people had "shotgun" weddings because a woman got pregnant before being married and it was considered a break with tradition. In many instances this still happens today. Getting married under this pretense for the sake of conforming to custom undermines our responsibility for making personal decisions.

GENERALLY, IF YOU want to join any organized group there are certain ceremonial rituals of initiation. For example, if you want to join a religious faith, then certain rituals need to be performed. If you want to join a social group, like a sorority, then you must go through secret rituals of initiation. The same is true for marriage. If you want to join the legions of respectable and mature adults, then it is the general belief that you need to be married. In our society, a relationship that doesn't reach the ultimate goal of marriage is seen as a failure.

Marriage is a rite of passage. It is a customary coming-of-age tradition in which a person feels inducted, and is perceived as being inducted, into adulthood. The social stigma attached to the idea of not being married is vital to a person's desire to be married in this society.

As the tradition of marriage is so engrained in the fabric of our lives and identities, similar to other rituals and traditions, we don't necessarily question it. Oftentimes we feel pressure because we believe it is the expected next step in our prescribed lives.

Everything in our culture, including our rituals and traditions, plays an important role in shaping our shared views and understanding of the world. By conforming to rituals, we feel more accepted and connected. Although we generally enjoy the connectedness we attain from our traditions, we also conform to them so we can belong. Marriage and having children is what we are told we are supposed to do if we want to live a happy, fulfilled life. It is the "grown up" thing we need to do to be considered an adult. And so we conform to what we believe is the path we must follow to be accepted and lead a "normal" life.

We are creatures of habit, but even more so, creatures of comfort. Rituals help us achieve routine, stability, and comfort in such an impermanent world. Our world, and life, changes so rapidly that the unpredictability of this change scares us, causing us to cling to anything that gives us a psychological sense of stability and continuity. Marriage provides us the framework of control and predictability. It gives a sense of security that our partners will stay emotionally and sexually committed to us until "death do us part." There is absolutely no guarantee that will happen, but we like to believe it because of the security that it gives us.

Our shared dream of marriage supercedes other aspects of our identity. It is embedded in our cultural rituals and traditions, becoming part of our social DNA. It isn't only a part of our cultural traditions from which we derive our sense of identity, but it is an aspect that is reinforced by our media. Through media, we are constantly being fed the narrative that a woman's destiny can only be fulfilled through marriage.

Social conditioning by means of the media starts even before we have had a chance to develop our identities. As children, we hear stories of the young princess who is saved by the handsome prince. From teenage years onward, we read magazines that feature relationship articles and quizzes. Beauty products for looking younger and sexier are marketed even to young girls. We are sold books and watch television shows that teach "how to get a man." Movies portray happily ever after romantic endings in which the girl always gets Prince Charming. We are reminded daily, through social media, about engagements, weddings, and girls marrying their "best friends" and living happily ever after. Weddings are glamorized on television. Images of marriages are everywhere. The inundation is constant and overwhelming.

Through this never-ending stream of information, we are told a woman derives personal fulfillment from marriage. The question becomes: Why? There is no doubt that the imagery of marriage in media sustains a multibillion-dollar industry, which contributes to the promotion of this message. However, we falsely believe that media drives our needs and desires. We accuse the media of propagating the images and the myth.

If we look deeper, beyond the commercial appeal of the media, we will see that media images are just reflections of what already exists in our minds. Marriage is part of our collective consciousness and the media is just reflecting that thinking. Media images only reinforce the need. They show us who we are, not who we want to be. Marketing and media images are designed to bypass the rational part of our thinking and appeal to our emotional side. And thus, the media only feeds our cravings.

Media may or may not always keep pace with the desires and needs of society. As we continue to evolve our thinking, we can anticipate that media will be more reflective of who we are.

New images have emerged and started to shape media imagery. We are starting to see traces of changing social mores and diversity in our current media. Media is beginning to reflect the "new normal" of what is acceptable ranging from homosexuality, singles living together, interracial coupling, and the successfully empowered heroine. Where we are now is a far cry from the 1950s, where the predominant image was that of the heterosexual nuclear family. This shift isn't because media drives our thinking, but because our thinking drives media. As we continue to evolve our thinking and change our desires, media, to the extent that it is a mirror, will follow. Therefore, in order to see the change we must be the change. That requires us to mentally shift our thinking about what we truly need to be happy. But first, we must find out what it is that truly makes us happy.

Rituals and traditions have a positive role in our lives. They are symbolic representations that help us celebrate the events of life. However, we shouldn't underestimate the role they play in shaping our beliefs, including what we believe to be socially acceptable.

What are the rituals and traditions that you hold near to your heart? How do they influence your beliefs? Do you use them to define your identity?

We cling to social conventions because of the sense of normalcy and connectedness to the larger world that we get from them. The tradition of marriage is no different. Like most of our rituals and traditions, we often feel it is what we are supposed to do. It is what our culture and families expect from us.

There is great comfort in surrendering our individual choices to past ideals to avoid personal responsibility for our actions. But there are ways in which we can preserve our customs without sacrificing our individual desires. To be free from the societal expectations of who we need to be, we need to relinquish the past. The ideology of *"It has always been done this way"* isn't acceptable in making decisions about our lives. We must make personalized decisions based on our current circumstances and what works best for us at the given time, no matter what. We aren't being served by all things at all times.

If something is not serving you, then let it go. You don't need to hold on to something that isn't working for you.

To do this we can establish the practice of mindful awareness. Little by little, all it takes is becoming more mindful of our habits, thoughts, rituals, and actions. When we cling to the idea that things ought to be a certain way, because tradition dictates it to be so, we should pause to better understand why we believe that to be true.

Is the belief that you cling to serving you? If it isn't, then let it go and replace it with something that does. By asking yourself these types of questions, what naturally occurs is you become more aware of what really matters in your life. And life becomes simpler.

CHAPTER 5
Religion

Be gentle, compassionate, and allow yourself to create the space you need to become deeply grounded within yourself. All it takes is accepting that you are a human who is evolving and discovering your true nature.

OUR RELIGIOUS BELIEFS and practices influence, and in many instances dictate, our thinking and behavior. In most religions, marriage is a fundamental ideal, making it a commonly shared belief that marriage is a sacred union that we should aspire to in our relationships. Our religions influence how we define marriage, who we can marry, the rights and obligations of spouses, and the legitimacy of divorce.

Of course, not everyone views life through the lens of religion. With a growing number of people who consider themselves eclectically spiritual, rather than traditionally religious, and who are establishing personalized spiritual practices for themselves, there is a shift from the concept that marriage is a religious act to a view that marriage is an agreement between two consenting adults.

Still, with an overwhelming majority of people participating in some form of organized religion, it impacts people's desire and decision to get married.

For many of us, religion is important because it helps us interpret the divine forces in our lives. It provides us with an understanding of the natural world. It is through our spiritual practice that we experience peace in such a chaotic world.

Many of our beliefs about marriage come from our religious teachings. For a long time I believed marriage was a sacrament between a man and a woman. I judged any other type of union contrary to my beliefs as being wrong. Intellectually I knew that any secular marriage, such as going to the court to get married, changed the status of a person just the same as anybody who goes to a church. But I believed otherwise. It troubled me that my beliefs were so rigid. I asked myself, *What makes my beliefs superior? What makes me right and everyone else wrong?*

We are personally liable for examining and stretching the limits of our beliefs to achieve what we have been put here for: to learn and grow. If you want to reach your full potential as a human being you have to investigate who you are and what you believe. If you don't, you end up becoming like so many other people, following patterns of habit. An unconscious being.

This can be challenging because there are a multitude of people telling us who we need to be and how we should live our lives, which clouds our understanding of who we truly are. The people who seem to feel strongest about how we should live our lives are religious fundamentalists. The judgment and criticisms of these people are unjustifiably critical of anything that deviates from their interpretation of life. If you have premarital sex or live with your boyfriend, you are living "in sin." You are condemned as "immoral" if you use birth control. If you get divorced, you are considered "depraved." If you love someone of the same sex, you are "going to hell." If your behavior doesn't fit squarely into the framework of their views, then you are considered immoral. Through this constant chastisement we are taught we are "good" only if we are obedient. For most of us, including these religious conservatives, who might never admit it, none of our lives fit into these perfect idealistic images. As a result, we struggle to conform to these beliefs.

We are conditioned by our religious beliefs to think that there is one path we must follow for love and family. If you are involved in a modern-day relationship, where you are having premarital sex or living with your partner, you might feel guilt for not being married.

For all intents and purposes, considering the growing gap between our traditional religious values and our real-world actions, marriage in the name of religion seems to be used predominantly to garner the approval of family members, friends, and society—people who believe that marriage is the right course of action. Many times we marry to placate our own biased belief systems, which tell us we need to marry for our relationships to be considered respectable.

How often do we hear stories about a couple being pressured into marriage by the partners' families? Take, for instance, a woman who comes from a very traditional family. She lives with her boyfriend and unexpectedly becomes pregnant. Her family is ashamed of her because she isn't married. To avoid being shamed by her family, the couple gets married to make an "honest woman of her."

Even if the couple had every intention of one day getting married, it wasn't of their own will that they got married. Rather, it is to accommodate their families' beliefs.

Our faiths don't permit us the ability to customize what marriage means to us. It teaches us there is a social order that one must follow to be considered righteous. We feel guilty if our life choices don't align with our spiritual beliefs. Our guilt, a derivative of our beliefs, causes us to default to what has been largely defined for us.

Granted, under the best circumstances we marry to formally recognize and assert our commitment publically. If we do so, then our actions and values are aligned.

This may very well be true, but there is a divide between our religious beliefs and everyday actions. Most of us consummate relationships long before we entertain the idea of marriage. It is typical for women today to be sexually active, engaging with multiple partners before marriage. It is common for us to live with our partners. We have children outside of marriage.

Even though there is a considerable disconnect between the realities we are living and the prescription of our religious doctrines, we cling to old beliefs. If our actions are a reflection of who we are and what we believe, then they serve as a silent objection to certain beliefs we hold. Yet, we haven't given ourselves the permission to live our lives to our choosing in light of how we are told we need to live.

Our actions show us that we intellectually realize we don't need marriage to form a spiritual bond with our partner. Either we have a spiritual bond with our partner or we don't. Marriage doesn't create or give us that. We can desire marriage, but we should accept that we don't need it to express our love for one another. Believing marriage is a necessity causes us to become dependent on it to nurture and preserve our relationships, rather than putting in the required effort to strengthen and grow our relationships. If we want to formally recognize our commitment through the act of marriage then we can. However, relinquishing our attachment to the idea that we must be married for love or to form a special bond frees us to seek out a true life partner, rather than trying to achieve a social ideal.

MARRIAGE IS REGARDED as sacred in religion, primarily to cultivate celibacy. That is, religion regulates sexuality through the institution of marriage. Chastity has been particularly pronounced in religion as it pertains to women. When we take a closer look, we typically see that mainstream thinking and socially accepted behavior is reflective of its cultural framework. For many years celibacy was birth control before birth control existed. Chastity and monogamy for women was vital to knowing who fathered a woman's child. As such, controlling women's sexuality was historically considered essential.

Until recently, women have been culturally deterred from engaging in premarital sex and needed the institution of marriage to comfortably explore and enjoy sex. Imagine how it must have felt to need marriage in order to experience something so natural and instinctive as sex. Although most of us today don't hold ourselves to the same standards, this thinking certainly has impacted our views on fulfilling our feminine identity, and contributed to our desire to get married. If we held ourselves to the same standard of waiting until marriage to enjoy the pleasures of sex, many of us wouldn't be engaging in sexual relations until we were well into our late twenties or early thirties. For many of us this is unrealistic.

Most women today don't practice abstinence before marriage. Today's women even celebrate our sexual emancipation. How do we reconcile our celebration of sexuality with our traditional religious beliefs, if they are at odds? Do we go back to a time when premarital sex and cohabitation were considered unacceptable? Do we forfeit having children because we don't marry until later in life? No. We should move forward to chart our own life courses. We can do so without dissolving our deepest values and the universal truths underlying our religious teachings: love, respect, forgiveness, equality, and nonjudgment.

The image of marriage that comes from our religious teachings in many instances need to be refreshed. We base our beliefs on patriarchal religions that were largely defined by men in the cultural framework of another era. Rather than blindly applying these teachings to the present day, it is important to understand the context of the times that justified the thinking so we can reject what no longer makes sense.

Religion has a lot to say about the role of women and marriage. Unfortunately, many religions are thematically repressive, advocating a woman's subordination and inferiority to men. Times are dramatically different since the formation of our early spiritual teachings. If we take a closer look, we will see a direct correlation between the thinking and the social, political, and economic events of those times. It doesn't mean all the beliefs our ancestors subscribed to are still applicable in modern times. But a good many of them deserve to be discarded—never to be recycled.

There seems to be a widely held belief that religion is set

in stone, protected by its antiquity, never to be challenged. It is a pity to think that the development of religion stopped centuries ago after scriptural texts memorialized religious doctrines. Are only events that predated these scriptures considered our religion? Can we be open to believing that our spiritual teachings aren't frozen in time, but are divinely imparted to us every day? Not wanting to evolve our religious practices is like not wanting to change laws established hundreds of years ago even if there is an obvious need for a change. As a people we are allowed to grow and get better. We don't have to be stuck in the past just for the sake of it. We have to examine these systems of thinking to figure out what makes the most sense currently for each of our lives.

In time, religions will refresh their views to better respond to the needs and people of today. There is too much at stake given the considerable amount of people that are alienated because religion isn't adaptive. The point isn't about forcing religious institutions to accept what they consider unacceptable. Rather, I look forward to the day religions are less judgmental and more open to the needs of the people they claim to serve. I will revel on the day that people whose beliefs are stagnant get unstuck, evolve their thinking, and stop trying to defend the norms of centuries past.

Religion understandably is a touchy subject because we are so passionate about, and partial to our own religious beliefs. Religion contains many gems of wisdom to help us live more meaningful lives. It reveals many truths to help us live better lives. If religion helps you foster a relationship with God then that is a beautiful thing. We all need to be grounded in something to grow. That may be religion for you. It is up to each of us to relate to the divine forces in our lives how we choose.

In light of your beliefs, can you find the spiritual space to discover your personal truth? Spiritual space is a place inside of you where you can be your true self with no boundaries, no beliefs, no guilt, and no judgment. It is creating an internal sanctuary where no one else is allowed or has access—not your mother, friends, pastor, teachers, no one. Create the space to be introspective. This practice of compassionately looking inward will help you discover the truths about yourself. As you gain more and more access to this space, you will learn to relax into that space to get a glimpse into the internal universe of your thoughts and feelings. When you are able to comfortably release into that space then you can begin to fill the space with all that is you. This is how you can become full-filled. Create spiritual space to commune with the divinity that lives within you to help guide you.

Ideally, the best way to access your spiritual space is through stillness. A still body creates a still mind. The opportunity to practice stillness is always available. Certainly, a great way to practice stillness is through meditation. If you don't practice meditation, then you can try another simple practice like to sit in bed an extra five minutes before you rise or go to sleep. Or if you have a regular practice of prayer you can extend that by a few minutes. Do whatever works best for you to achieve stillness in your life. Through the practice of stillness you will begin to develop a deeper relationship with yourself. Can you be silent? Can you be still to hear the wisdom that lives within you?

Many of us experience guilt when questioning our spiritual beliefs. You don't have to be so hard on yourself. Be gentle, compassionate, and allow yourself to create the space you need to become deeply grounded within yourself. All it takes is accepting that you are a human who is evolving and discovering your true nature. Just as a child in her innocence doesn't feel guilty to ask questions to understand life and divinity, so too can you create a safe harbor to examine your beliefs. Dwelling in that space will help you to find balance in your thoughts, and in turn, the way you view the world and your life. When you operate in this manner, you become more conscious. Allow yourself the freedom to move, grow, and change at all times.

CHAPTER 6
Mothering

*You have to claim your power and determine what you want
your life to look like in the short time you get to spend here.
No one has the right to live your life for you. Only you can
give away or claim that power.*

AS HUMANS, we have two basic instincts: survival and procreation.

As women, we were created with the exclusive ability to
gestate and birth children. It is our right to have children if we
are fortunate enough to conceive and want to have them.

The reality is that if you want children then you have a
biological imperative to have them by a certain age. Having
children isn't something that can be indefinitely deferred like
the long-awaited vacation to Paris you have been putting off.
Unfortunately, it is a decision that must be made at a less con-
venient time in a woman's life, such as when she is working
on her career or pursuing higher education. In our changing
world, where women can live as freely as we want, the idea of
independence is less attractive to a woman who desires to be in
a partnership to have children.

Although we can't overlook the fact that some women marry later in life, women are powerfully motivated to marry during their reproductive years. It is a contributing factor as to why women may desire marriage sooner than men. Men don't have the same pressures or worries about the age at which they conceive a child. Their biology allows them to have children at almost any age. Unfortunately, for women this isn't the case. We can become parents through surrogacy or adoption outside of our reproductive years, but if we wish to birth a baby, there is a finite window of opportunity. This is our reality.

As we continue to take on larger roles outside of the home, the trade-off of waiting to marry is pushing our focus on having children to later in life. Once a woman reaches a certain age, the reality of how difficult it can be to conceive a child emerges and becomes more pronounced. Admittedly, if a woman has made the decision to postpone having a child in lieu of seeking personal independence, financial stability, career advancement, or waiting to find the right partner, it seems unfair that she be penalized in such a way. But regardless of how she may feel, that is our biological reality.

Never before have we been empowered to own our decisions for mothering. The modern woman has options. If you believe you are constrained by your biological clock, then you will be. Alternatives now exist if you are willing to do what it takes. Although we will forever be bound to the reality of when we have children, we have options. If we clearly see our choices then that enables us to make deliberate decisions and have no regrets because we weighed all the options.

The advancements of modern medicine, which contribute to the betterment of lives every day, have granted women the ability to extend their child-bearing years to a degree. Medical advancements, such as embryo and egg freezing, are relatively new options that accommodate the modern woman, giving her the ability to temporarily defer pregnancy, so she may, for instance, pursue a higher level of education, advance her career, or become better established. Having these options reduces the pressure to forgo pursuing our goals for fear of sacrificing our opportunity to bear children. Having the capacity to be deliberate in our timing and decision to mother is liberating.

We are fortunate to be women living in our times. A lot more fortunate than the women of the past. To the extent we need to, we should take full advantage of these advancements for mothering. If you were a woman living in the 1960s and chose to wait later in life to have children, you forfeited your opportunity. Even women as recent as the last 15 to 20 years didn't have the luxury to wait to have children. These medical advances were born out of necessity of our changing society. As our needs evolve, we must be able to keep pace with our social evolution. We can be more purposeful in living full lives to the extent we are open to new realities.

We aren't always willing to embrace change. Change in our behavior, thinking, and acceptance of new norms is slow. Generally it takes time for our thinking to keep pace with our changing world. Typically, generations that are brave enough to challenge the norm do so because they were born into different circumstances. They are adapting to the changing conditions around them. It has taken the bold efforts of several successive generations to begin to overcome archaic, discriminatory practices such as racism and sexism. Culturally we are a work in progress when it comes to tolerance and change.

Although medical alternatives for natural impregnation may seem unconventional and strange, in the future this will likely be the new normal. Because of how full women's lives are, and will continue to be, it will be considered normal for women to elect alternative ways of extending their fertile years to become mothers. As the cost of fertility procedures decline and become more financially viable, as institutions recognize the importance of providing coverage for these elective procedures, and as more and more women continue to pursue excellence in their lives, we will undoubtedly see a rise in the number of women electing these options. The women of the next generation will be more adaptive to their circumstances and likely won't think twice about electing procedures to extend their fertility, such as preserving their eggs. In the future, women will come to embrace these alternatives in a manner similar to how our generation embraces birth control.

IT IS PART of our collective consciousness to believe that marriage is necessary to have children. Wanting children factors into our desire for marriage. Many of us want to have children with a long-term partner we love and respect. There is certainly value in raising a child together with a partner, such as sharing child-rearing responsibilities and giving the child a chance to regularly foster deep relationship with both parents.

But if you are close to reaching your reproductive maturity and want to have a child, then why not? We are biologically disposed to have children, so why do we believe we can only have them if we are married? The thought that we need marriage to have children is a limitation created by our beliefs. In many instances, our misguided beliefs prevent us from living the lives we want. Sure you may want to be married to raise a child, but you certainly don't have to be.

Social convention dictates it is the normal path to get married and then have children. There is the idea that marriage creates a more stable environment for a child, and that, children are likelier to be healthier and happier if they are raised by two full-time committed parents living under the same roof. Whether or not this is true, this belief is typically based on one's personal experience. A person raised in a two-parent household, or who has strong religious views, or who had a negative experience living in a single-parent home and believes they were lacking something because they didn't have the attention of both parents may all share this view.

We only know what we know. There is no way you can fully understand a reality that you didn't personally experience. If you were raised by a single parent, you don't know the realities of what it would have been like to be raised by both of your parents to know whether or not your life would have been better—you just believe you do. On the contrary, if you grew up with both of your parents then you don't know what it was like to grow up in a single-parent household. It doesn't matter what you saw on television, how often you got a glimpse into your friends' family life, or if people shared their experiences with you. Those are their personal experiences and have nothing to do with you and your experience. Even if you were put in the same situation as them there is no telling what your experience would have been.

We wrongfully assume our experiences are a fair representation of the rest of the world. We view the world through these blinders and use them to interpret and understand life. But we are bound by our personal experiences. I may try to empathize about growing up in a single-parent household, but I am limited in my understanding because that wasn't my reality. It would be self-important of me to pretend to know someone's experience that is dissimilar to mine.

When we are aware that we interpret life through the filter of our own experiences we begin to develop an appreciation for multiple realities. We realize that our lives don't have to be limited by our beliefs.

Your assumptions and beliefs about someone else's experience don't make it the truth. For a long time, I believed that because I grew up in a loving two-parent household it was the only way a family could be happy. I was blinded by my personal experience. When I was able to suspend my beliefs and speak with people who were raised in a healthy and loving single-parent household I learned that my assumptions weren't accurate. As I have now come to understand, our beliefs serve as our truth, not *the truth*. Plenty of children who are happy and later grow up to be successful are raised by single parents—and not just by women, but also by men. The belief that marriage is necessary to raise a healthy, happy, and successful child is true only because we believe it to be true. The idea that we need marriage to have a child comes from the larger construct that our lives must look a certain way.

The reality is that many children are being raised in single-parent households. There are many parents who were married and are now separated, raising their children on their own. There are many husbands and wives who are widowed and faced with the task of raising their children by themselves. There are many people whose spouses are overseas serving their country in the military or traveling for work to support their family, who are raising their children on their own. Despite the circumstances, these people are doing an exceptional job of raising healthy and happy children.

Marriage doesn't guarantee that a child will have a healthy and happy upbringing. There are plenty of children who grow up in an unhealthy, abusive, and destructive household consisting of married parents. Are we to assume that they are healthy and happy?

It is hard to break free from these indoctrinations because they are a part of our collective consciousness. The belief that we can only have children within marriage is nothing but a self-imposed limitation. We have confined ourselves to one path, which gives us less and less options.

Many of our beliefs about marriage and family are the result of the stigmas of being a single mother and having "illegitimate" children. Women who have a child outside of marriage are judged. Historically, the children of unwed mothers were considered illegitimate. An unwed mother was alienated and faced severe social repercussions, while children born out of wedlock didn't have the same rights as other children. The judgments about having a child outside of marriage can be crippling to the psyche, causing us to desire marriage to have children.

Stigmas about women who don't have children also causes women angst. Because of the shared belief that women should have children, those who don't have any often feel shamefully stripped of their feminine identity. This can be very painful and cause pressure on us to conform to this socially dictated norm. If you are one of these women, you might start to believe something is wrong with you because you aren't like other women.

But you get to choose how you want to live your life. You can't forgo living your life in loyalty to an ideology.

Having children is a choice. You may decide you don't want to have children. You may decide that you don't want to go it alone, which of course is perfectly okay. It is by no means an easy task to be a parent. Of course, anything in life worth having requires hard work. If you feel you need to be married to have a child, then by all means you should pursue that path. There is certainly some value, both for parent and child. But if you want to fulfill your dream of motherhood and believe you can successfully raise a child singlehandedly, then you have options. If you can't afford to prolong having a child and are emotionally and financially stable, you have the option of choosing to raise a child on your own through adoption, insemination, or finding a suitable partner to agree to father your child.

We have options, and more importantly, choices. Our choices empower us to chart the course of our lives. Having the ability to control our bodies and reproductive systems has liberated us. If we limit our choices because of our controlled way of thinking or fear of people's opinions then we disempower ourselves. We should step beyond that which we believe to be true and make the decisions that best reflect our desires and our own personal realities.

Everything in life is a choice. Your evolution begins with your power of choice. It begins with the understanding that what you choose to believe controls your life. The limitation of your beliefs is enough to render you powerless. Anytime you feel like you have no options it is because you have placed limits on your power of choice. It isn't for lack of having choices.

You have to claim your power and determine what you want

your life to look like in the short time you get to spend here. No one has the right to live your life for you. Only you can give away or claim that power. You give away that right when you don't exercise your power of choice. If you give away that power, you are complicit in allowing it to happen. We shouldn't sacrifice living our lives for the sake of achieving an ideal of what is acceptable in the eyes of others. Are you willing to let go of your deeply held beliefs in order to achieve personal freedom?

You have many options if you are willing to see past how you think things "should be." You are only as liberated as you believe yourself to be. You don't have to sacrifice your choices for mothering on the altar of a traditional belief system.

—— **PART III** ——

Psychological
Influences

CHAPTER 7
The Finger of Illusion

When you are able to free yourself from the idea that life is a fairytale, then you will be able to change the way you view yourself and the world.

WE ALL KNOW the story of happily ever after. The story always begins, "Once upon a time." The story always ends, "And they lived happily ever after. The End."

The story always conveniently ends with a happy couple riding off into the sunset and we never hear what happens afterwards because it is assumed they live happily ever after. In reality, the story never ends there. It has actually just begun. For some reason, however, we aren't taught to envision that part of the story.

By conveniently ending the story with happily ever after, it adheres to the cultural myth that once we fall in love and get married we are guaranteed a life of endless happiness. The glorified romanticism of marriage compels us to long for the fantasy. Women who aren't married aspire to obtain it. Those who are married strive to preserve it.

The story of happily ever after isn't completely dismissive though. It reveals a lot to us about what we ultimately desire: to be happy. Life is tough. Fairy tales give us a sense of hope in a world of suffering and uncertainty. Who wouldn't want a perfect fairy tale ending? No one would vote for an imperfect life, yet that too often is our reality. The desire to marry and live "happily ever after" reveals that we are ultimately in search for happiness. We have just agreed that there is one path for finding it.

If we do try to imagine married life, we often labor under the misapprehension that marriage and our partner will cure all our problems. This idea that we can achieve personal fulfillment through marriage makes us feel that we will be better off if we find Prince Charming and get married. We believe marriage to be like the fairy tales that tell us it is the fountain of endless happiness. In Fantasy Land, there is the wish to be saved by a handsome knight. So we hope and dream to be rescued. But rescued from what? Rescued from a life that somehow may not look like everyone else's? Rescued from a life of not being good enough? Rescued from having no identity?

For all our lives, we have consumed the same message that marriage is our happily ever after. It is the story we are taught from the earliest age. From a very early age, girls dream of being swept off their feet. Have you ever dreamed of being swept off your feet or fantasized about Prince Charming? Personally, I have heard many women say they have dreamed of their wedding day since they were little girls. Little boys don't seem to have those same dreams about marriage. As boys grow into men, they may have the desire to find good wives and have children, but they don't have the same "I'm waiting for my savior" fantasy that women do. In fact, most men talk about marriage in the context of "settling down."

We accept the myth of happily ever after as our truth. Unfortunately, the "happily ever after" fantasy isn't a self-fulfilling prophecy. Can you honestly say that you know of anyone whose marriage can accurately be described as "happily ever after?" Even if you are able to think of someone who has a healthy and happy relationship, I am sure they wouldn't describe their relationship in these terms. If you talk to any married person she will confirm that marriage can be one of the greatest bonds shared between two people, but requires constant effort. "Happily ever after" implies effortlessness and a guarantee of never-ending bliss. This is simply not possible, as all meaningful relationships require work. The true definition of love is when two people are willing to work at making each other happy—together. It is through this work that we demonstrate our love.

Any married person will tell you that among the happy times there are periods of sadness, loneliness, and frustration, even in the greatest of relationships. There are, of course, those who would have you believe that their lives are perfect. But you must remember, it is most people's goal to convince you how great their lives are. To wear a good mask. If you observe, most people aren't even honest with themselves. So how could they be honest with you? People who feel the need to boast about their wonderful, perfect lives are typically trying to convince themselves more than you.

Our expectations of marriage as an effortless, unending source of happiness are unrealistic. This doesn't mean we can't experience happiness in a relationship. It only means happiness isn't contingent on a relationship. If you believe that marriage automatically leads to happily ever after, then study the rates of divorce and infidelity. The statistics might sober you up. If we have unrealistic expectations of marriage we may be disappointed because we are hoping to experience a fairy tale, which doesn't necessarily lead us to what we ultimately desire: happiness.

There is a collective belief that by a certain age we should be married. Once we turn a certain age, which varies by culture, the tides of fear slowly start to rise until we feel we can hardly keep our head above water. It causes mounting stress and unnecessary pressure if you aren't going along with what your peers are doing. Fear starts to settle in, and you worry that your life might not be what you hoped for.

Society often gives us a very narrow view of what is and isn't acceptable. It tells us that a good life is shaped in a certain way. If you follow a certain path, then you are normal and acceptable. If you get married, you are righteous and promised never-ending happiness. If you do anything contrary to following the prescribed path, then you aren't guaranteed to be happy. Most of us want to be recognized as normal and seen as worthy, so we accept this as the truth. However, the concept of the endless happy marriage is a myth that has become part of our collective consciousness. So powerful it manipulates our dreams.

We use our belief system to interpret our experiences and define who we are and how we should live our lives. And through our belief system, we have come to an agreement with society, ourselves, family, and friends that marriage is good, right, and a necessary step in one's life. Most of us go a step further and add colorful dimensions to our beliefs about marriage, such as: "*I need to be married before I'm 30,*" "*I will only marry someone with a certain amount of wealth," "I can't marry someone who doesn't practice the same religious faith as me."*

When we take a close look at the conditions of our beliefs we see they are full of illusions. At our most basic level we don't need these things to be happy. It is the ego, the part of our psyche that is hyper-obsessed with our self-importance, which needs these things.

Can you imagine if you had no preconceived notions about how your life should be? Envision what your life would look like if you had no expectations of who you think you should be. If you had no beliefs about how you should look. No expectations of what it means to be a woman. No views of when you should be married. Or what you need to accomplish by a certain age. When we let go of the illusions of our beliefs, we free ourselves to enjoy life more fully.

Often our beliefs imprison us by limiting our freedom of choice.

When you cling to the belief that your life has to look a particular way or follow a certain path, you are inevitably going to be unhappy when reality contradicts your ideal. Life is going to happen the way it happens, which doesn't always go according to plan. That is a fact. You prevent yourself from experiencing true happiness if you adhere too rigidly to a plan because anything that deviates from your defined path will bother you. When you become narrowly fixated on achieving a specific outcome, you close yourself off to all the other possibilities.

If you don't hold the belief that there is some magical yellow brick road that leads to a fantasy destination at the end of your journey, then you are likely to remain free of unrealistic expectations. Many of us are busy clinging to false ideals that we aren't able to really enjoy life.

Sometimes we get stuck in a perpetual state of not feeling whole. We internalize an ideal to such an extent that it becomes toxic. It takes control of our actions, emotions, thoughts, appearance, and everything in our lives. The loss of control causes us to live in a constant state of anxiety and fear. The thinking is, "*What will become of me?*"

As an example, you go on a social network and see that one of your friends recently got engaged. You desperately want to be happy for her, but for a second your heart stops beating and your gut feels hollow because you wish it were you. You worry and silently ask yourself, "*When will it be me? I've been patient. I've been good. Why not me?*" Without even knowing it, you are consumed by doubts about your identity. In a split second, you are transported to a tragic place with just you and the thought, "*I may never fulfill my dreams.*"

This happens so often in our lives. We aren't enjoying a night out with friends because we are so worried about meeting someone. We aren't celebrating New Year's because we think we somehow lost out during the previous year. We don't feel fortunate or excited turning another year older because we believe time is "running out." Often, if we are in a relationship, we aren't even enjoying the love we share with our partner because of our wish to obtain the dream of marriage.

Guess what happens while all of this takes place? Life happens. It doesn't wait for you while you complain about what you don't have or what you wish you had. Rather, it continues on its course. As you are distracting yourself from all that is and all that could be, you miss out.

When I think of all the women I know, myself included, who have spent countless hours worried about finding a partner I realize that no matter how much energy is spent worrying or complaining, it never changes the situation or outcome. Later, many women wish they could get back the wasted time of regret to be more productive, to be fully engaged in all of those great moments, and just to be happy.

We may spend countless hours worrying about following the predefined life plan. We may expend countless hours unhappy if we haven't achieved this status quo. Worry creates anxiety and unhappiness, it never resolves anything.

Have you ever wondered why time seems to fly by so quickly? For many of us, it is because we aren't present and enjoying our current experiences. We are blindly counting down the days waiting for something different to happen to us so that "our lives can start." We are waiting for the moment when we get the right job, live in our dream house, make a certain amount of money, or find "Mr. Right" all at the expense of appreciating what we do have. If you don't want to see your life flash before your eyes then you must surrender the fears of your expectations to the uncertainty of the future.

Think about all the experiences that have led you to this very moment in your life. Could you, and did you, predict any of them? No. There are so many forces at play that are far beyond our conscious awareness. It is our job to be ready for life's experiences, not to worry about them.

One of the best ways to prepare yourself for what life has in store for you is getting to know yourself better.

Self-discovery helps us uncover our true essence and complete the circle of Self. We spend a lot of time learning the needs and desires of others, but a fraction of the time getting to know the person we spend the most amount of time with, ourselves.

Introspection is a practice. It is something we can introduce into our lives on a daily basis. To get to know yourself better you can playfully experiment. Experiment with changing your habits, as an example. If you are used to looking in the mirror and always finding something wrong with your appearance, perhaps the next time you look into the mirror give yourself a compliment. Find out what happens. How did you feel? Was it difficult, and if so why?

Self-study also naturally happens when we do the things we love. Find something you love to do to engage yourself in life. It can be running, yoga, mentoring, playing a sport, volunteering, reading, anything. Ultimately, when you do the things you love, you are more engaged in the present moment. It is in these moments that you learn about yourself. You learn about the strength you need to persevere, you become familiar with your habitual thoughts, you discover what it takes to relax and be yourself.

There are paths that can lead you to free yourself from your attachments to fantasy images so you can seek out love for better, more authentic reasons. When you are able to free yourself from the idea that life is a fairy tale, then you will be able to change the way you view yourself and the world. You will be able to make clear conscious choices for yourself, and choose to live your life according to you, and only you. You will become the narrator of your own story.

CHAPTER 8
The Experience of Feeling

Anytime someone believes you should live your life a certain way, that person is trying to live through you. It isn't at all about you. Through you, people increase their sense of self. It is purely about them.

FEELINGS ARE UNIVERSAL. As humans we all experience the same feelings: happiness, sadness, jealousy, anger, ecstasy, and fear.

Feelings are a form of self-expression. In spite of what anyone tells you, your feelings matter. It isn't your job, or anyone else's, to minimize the experience of your emotions or feelings. Others might try to convince you that your feelings don't matter or are insignificant. They may tell you that you should just be happy for all that you have. This may very well be true, but it doesn't diminish the experience of your feelings.

Feelings are one of our greatest teachers about humanity. For this reason, they should be acknowledged. Once you have experienced certain feelings, you are better able to relate to others who are experiencing that same feeling. Feelings allow us to be more compassionate, understanding, and connected to those around us. For example, after my heart was broken I was more empathetic and understanding of others who were mending broken hearts. I knew what it felt like.

Our emotions, which are activated by the sensations in our bodies—our feelings—are typically triggered by an underlying cause. But we are often so consumed by our feelings without knowing why. For instance, take a woman who is jealous anytime her boyfriend talks to another woman. This woman is so consumed with her jealousy that she doesn't realize her feelings are caused by her insecurity about herself. No relationship will give her a sense of security until she understands the cause of her feelings and works on self-love.

Often we experience the feelings of anxiety, fear, or despair if our lives aren't aligned with our expectations. To better understand this, let's experiment. If you can, picture your future self—simply fast forward your life ten years. Suppose that you are successful and have accomplished many professional aspirations. You live in a beautiful home. You have great friends, a harmonious family, and an active social life. You are healthy. Life is good. However, you are *not* married. Let's say that you want kids one day, but you are doubtful this is ever going to happen because you are getting older and don't have a serious partner. You would have thought by now that after patiently waiting, praying, and doing everything you have been advised that you would have met your perfect match.

How would you feel about that?

Possibly some of the following feelings come to mind: loneliness, shame, fear, inadequacy, or unworthiness. You may question what it says about you that you cannot find the love you seek. Perhaps it means you aren't worthy of a meaningful relationship.

We often try to cover up our unpleasant feelings. Or we feel guilty about having these feelings. You should never feel bad about your feelings. By feeling bad you are punishing yourself twice. You not only feel bad, but now you feel bad about feeling bad. There is no justice in that for you. If you experience an unpleasant feeling, like loneliness or sadness, simply acknowledge what you are feeling. You don't have to punish yourself for experiencing your emotions.

I am not sure why we are so adamant about suppressing our feelings. Who among us hasn't experienced unpleasant feelings? So why are we ashamed to acknowledge them? If we acknowledge and confront our feelings, we can better understand what is causing them. When we close ourselves off to experience our feelings we prevent ourselves from understanding who we are.

Every feeling is motivated by a thought. Every thought is supported by a belief. It is our responsibility to understand the experience of our feelings. To deny any feeling is to deny your thoughts. When we deny our thoughts we only hinder our evolution because we keep ourselves from understanding the different aspects of who we are.

In your mind, you likely hold an image of what you believe to be your perfect life. For many women, part of that image centers on marriage and children. You have likely been taught that marriage and kids is the next and necessary step in your life. That it is a source of happiness and well-being. We fear we won't live up to being the perfect selves that we have created in our mind's eye. We believe that we won't please or be accepted by others. The thought of living unattached creates a lot of suffering. It is shameful to think we aren't good enough for someone to love us. Eventually we start to believe that this may be true.

Fear eventually takes over and becomes the driving force behind our actions. You might be in an unfulfilling relationship with someone that you really don't like to preserve your self-importance. You may not love your partner, but it might give you a sense of comfort to tell everyone that you are in a relationship. You might force yourself to marry someone to prove something to yourself and the rest of the world, instead of waiting for someone who is a better match for you, a true companion. These relationships usually falter because they are formed out of shallowness or ego.

The fear that our lives can't be complete without following a prescribed life plan generates unhappiness. We worry that we aren't pretty enough or good enough and that something must be wrong with us. Unfortunately, we are leaving it up to external sources to validate our being. There is nothing outside of our inner being that can give us a sense of *self*. The belief that we can derive a self from anything external to us is the biggest lie we believe.

You, and those in your life, may believe that your happiness is inextricably tied to someone else's acceptance of you. Finding someone who will "marry us" is a source of acceptance. We learn from a very early age the false need to be accepted. We want people to accept us because that gives us a sense of satisfaction that just maybe we are okay. We live in a world where we constantly seek acceptance and approval from others, but we can't forget we also live in a world full of judgment.

In order to evolve who you are, you must ask yourself questions about what you want and why.

Why do you want to get married?

Why do you walk on eggshells hoping he likes you?

What scares you about ending an unhealthy relationship?

If you never married, could you be happy?

Why do you want children?

Dare to ask yourself these questions, whichever ones are applicable. Are you scared to be alone? Do you feel happier when you are in a relationship? Will it please your family? Do you want companionship? Will it give you a sense of normalcy? Do you believe it is the expected next step in your life? What is it?

Really reflect on your answers. When you are able to honestly answer these questions you will uncover many truths about who you are. You may discover much you didn't know about yourself.

Everyone's answers will be different.

No matter what, you must be completely honest with yourself. This is a private quiz. No one is going to judge your answer. Your answers are for you and you alone. Most importantly, free yourself from judging your answer. The purpose here isn't to critique the answer, but to uncover your personal truth and gain awareness of your underlying beliefs and thoughts.

Most of the time, what I have observed is that desire is a reflection of some deeper part of us. Like the girl who is jealous anytime her boyfriend speaks to another woman, her need to control her boyfriend and their relationship is a reflection of her insecurity.

When I asked myself the question of why I wanted to get married, what I found was I desired marriage for acceptance and to feel whole. I believed marriage would prove to the world that I was a worthy woman. When I realized this, I uncovered that I needed to work on my self-acceptance.

The journey of self-acceptance begins when you embrace the idea that you are a unique being created like no other. You will never be like anyone else in this entire universe or lifetime. When you are able to embrace this truth you will begin to accept how great it is to be you. Your resilience will shine through even when you are faced with a difficult situation. Once I was able to do my inner work, it freed me from my selfish and superficial needs to find a partner.

Ask yourself questions. Find out who you are and what your work is. Once you do your work, like I did mine, you will become free from your emotional longing, expectations, and attachments to certain ideals. Instead, you will operate from a space of love, wisdom, and truth.

THERE IS A lot of external pressure for us to live our lives in a prescribed way. Does it feel like people are always trying to "fix" your life? Do they believe they know what is best for you or what will make you happy?

All of these voices cause us to experience self-doubt. When others meddle in our lives, for a few moments and maybe longer, our internal world crashes and our heart sinks. You may feel ashamed and embarrassed because it feels like an indictment on your life. You contemplate your life and start to worry. Eventually, you come to the conclusion that you aren't good enough. The internal monologue taking place in your head then distracts you from everything else going on around you.

Have you ever considered why these feelings of self-doubt are triggered? Is it because someone has expressed an opinion about how you should be living your life? Is it because someone has offered to help you solve your "life's problem"? That could be a part of it, but certainly not all of it. That isn't what is causing the disturbance inside of you.

For years, I didn't understand why it caused me so much pain when someone probed into my life. That's because I was focused on my emotions and not the underlying cause of my agony.

People's interference in my life only triggered my painful belief that I wasn't enough. They only touched a soft spot that already existed. The simple truth was that I, myself, believed I wasn't enough. The experience of my unhappiness was my need to feel worthy. This forced me to confront my belief that I wasn't good enough.

Owning our feelings, rather than making other people responsible for our feelings, is vital to our evolution. To achieve this we must understand what causes our feelings. When we experientially practice understanding and owning our feelings we become enlightened about our personal truths. We can do this in our daily lives by paying closer attention to our mental and physical reactions to certain situations.

Try something. Observe how you feel the next time someone tries to "fix" your life. Where is your energy drawn? Do you feel sad, withdrawn, or get defensive? What physical reactions are triggered within your body? Do you sweat, get flushed, or develop a headache? Make friends with whatever feelings arise to understand what is causing the feeling.

IT IS A well-known phenomenon that people project their beliefs, dreams, and desires on others. Even more startling of a phenomenon, however, is our willingness to allow others to do so.

People have a need for power and control. They want to influence and control not only their lives, but the lives of those around them. It helps them justify and give meaning to their own lives. It makes them feel more righteous about who they are, what they believe, and how they chose to live their lives. We all do this, including me and you.

People view the world through the prism of their beliefs and then try to impose them on everyone. This is why there is so much division and conflict in the world. Throughout time people have been persecuted because of a difference of belief. Each group believing they are right and trying to impose their will.

The same applies to people who try to force you to live your life a certain way. People falsely think what makes *them* happy is going to make *you* happy. We personalize *their* beliefs and then we suffer. They believe that the only way you can be happy is if your life looks like theirs. It is simply not true, but it is what people believe. Anytime someone believes you should live your life a certain way, that person is trying to live through you. It isn't at all about you. Through you, people increase their sense of self. It is purely about them. Their needs. Their desires. Their beliefs. Their dreams.

If you are aware that this happens you become less vulnerable. It won't stop people from projecting their beliefs on to you. But if you can remember this, then you can become immune to people's expectations and beliefs about how you should be living your life. What works for them isn't necessarily going to work for you. This gives you the freedom to better enjoy *your* experience of life instead of experiencing your life through their eyes. There is true liberation in that.

You will never be able to please everyone. If you waste your time trying to please everyone you will never be happy. They will never be satisfied. Even once you think you have made these third parties happy they can still be critical. I know of many young adults who get pressure from their families to get married. Then one day they meet someone special who they want to marry and their family still isn't happy and criticizes, "*He is too young,*" "*He isn't attractive enough,*" "*He doesn't make enough money,*" "*He isn't of a certain race / religion,*" and so on and so on. If you want to be at peace, then spend your energy pleasing yourself. You will feel more fulfilled.

People have a dream of the world that they cling to so strongly that they can't see past anything that deviates from their dream. As a result, they believe that you should be living your life according to the life they have defined for themselves. So remember: They are not *you* and you are not them! There is only one way to live your life—your way.

The truth is that people don't even realize what they are doing, so don't blame them. They think they have your best interest at heart and don't understand how hurtful their behavior may be. Sure they want you to be happy, but they want you to be happy how they think you should be happy. Not the way you need to be happy. It is quite ironic that they think they are helping you find happiness, but can contribute to your current state of unhappiness. Be aware that it happens and don't get caught in someone else's dreams so much that it taints your own.

If you want inner peace stop listening to everyone, especially when it pertains to how you should live your life or what is going to make you happy. No one has it all figured out. People don't know any better than you, and they certainly don't know what is best for you. *You do.*

Once you stop listening to everyone and start cultivating the voice inside of you, you will see your life transform. You will start living for you, and not for others. You will feel like an individual who is able to fulfill her purpose because you follow your intuition rather than being led by external forces. Along your journey you will make mistakes and might even get hurt. This is a fact of life that you may have to face, with or without everyone else's opinion. So why not do it your way?

Another aspect of achieving harmony in your life is to make the conscious decision not to define yourself with labels. You can do this by accepting that your life is a set of experiences, not labels. We mistakenly use labels as building blocks to define who we are, inconveniently painting ourselves into a box. As an example, suppose you are divorced. If you are divorced, remember that it isn't who you are. Divorce is an experience. But if you always define yourself with the label of being divorced then you subtly enter into an agreement with the expectations of the label. You might believe there are certain things that a divorced person should and shouldn't do. You live your life as a "divorced person" when you should be free to live your life as a person who has experienced certain life changes.

The same is true with the labels of single and married. These are just a different set of experiences. Your life isn't about labels. Every experience is distinct and worth living. Get rid of all your labels and honor your experience.

Lastly, there is no need to defend your life choices to anyone, including you. We try to make ourselves feel better about our lives by attempting to convince others. When we feel the need to justify ourselves to others it is our way of rationalizing with ourselves. We are trying to convince ourselves that our lives are complete. But there is absolutely no need. If you are complete, then you are complete. No convincing or justifications required. If you see your life as it is, not through the lens of prescribed social norms or labels then you won't need to waste time trying to justify yourself to others. Rather, you will realize your endless possibilities. And appreciate how great it is to be you.

CHAPTER 9
Projecting into the Future

If we develop a conclusion of how things should be we create blockages in our journey instead of allowing our lives to unfold naturally.

WHETHER WE KNOW it or not, we spend much of our time fantasizing about the future. We create mental images of who we expect we will be in the future, and then project those images.

In our minds, we create a clear image of what our future lives will be. We imagine who we will be, what we will look like, what we will think, where we will live, what job we will have, how much money we will earn, who our children will be, and so forth. We use these projections to make us feel more secure and in control of our lives, but it only creates more fear. We fear not living up to those images. We get so invested in these future selves that we aren't living in the present.

If you have a defined image of what your life should look like, then you are in a constant battle with this projected image because you are either trying to achieve the image or worried about not attaining the image. If we develop a conclusion of how things should be we create blockages in our journey instead of allowing our lives to unfold naturally. There is no harm in envisioning a dream for the future. However, we shouldn't become attached to a specific outcome because we don't know what the future holds. Anything could happen.

The flaw in creating a future self is that these imaginary projections are based on who we are and what we want today. We are unable to imagine that our future selves will be vastly different from our current selves. This is why adolescent years can be so tumultuous. Teenagers find it difficult to see past their current existences and believe that life as they know it today is how it is always going to be. Even if you talk to adults many will tell you, *"I am nothing like I was ten years ago. I have matured and now I know who I am."* Regardless of age, it is illogical to believe that who we will be tomorrow is the same as who we are today. The proof of this is your own life.

Who you were in the past isn't who you are today. Time is transformative. If you look back over the span of the last ten years, haven't your tastes, thoughts, beliefs, preferences, and outlooks changed? If so, then logically who you are today won't be who you are in the future either. It is difficult for us to accurately predict our future lives. As a result, we are relegated to believing that our past is a predictor of our future.

Although you may have a vision of your future based on your desires of today, those desires will most likely change because you will be a different person in the future. The idea that who we are right now is who we will be for the rest of our lives is what psychologists have coined the "end of history illusion."[1]

Life is constantly changing. We shouldn't get trapped in the illusion of the future because everything is subject to change. Even if you could envision your life a few years from now, the universe has a far greater plan for you than you could ever imagine.

As an example, say that your dream is to live and work internationally. You mentally project what your life will look like living in a new country: where you will be living, what you will be doing, your new friends, the restaurants you will be dining at, and so forth. You then become consumed with thoughts of living overseas and become frustrated if you aren't making progress towards that goal. As a result you become resentful towards your current job, coworkers, family, and friends. You spend an inordinate amount of time and energy fearing you will never realize your dreams. Anything that occurs that isn't according to your plan causes you upset.

However, a year from now you have fallen in love and want to start a family, which means working internationally is no longer a priority. You are a different person with a new set of priorities and desires. All the unnecessary suffering you experienced was only the result of entertaining your projected future self.

Given the societal expectations on women to follow the life plan of marriage and children, we tend to project images of our future married selves. It is our perfect self, living in a beautiful house with a perfect spouse and children. We form a vision of how we think our lives should be and then we live out these alternate realities in our minds. If we don't see signs of progress, we panic and fear we are running out of time. If we don't see manifestations of our imaginary lives in the imaginary timelines we created, we feel we are going to be left behind.

We may fear that others will find love and happiness and leave us behind. If so, remember that happiness isn't a zero-sum game. One person's gain doesn't equate to another person's loss. This means everyone can be blissfully happy simultaneously. There is no scarcity of happiness or love. It isn't rationed. If you think it is, this is because you fear that you aren't good enough to get a slice of the pie. It is nothing other than a self-imposed limitation.

Much of our fears stem from the creation of a future self, which is designed around our current conditions and desires. Not the desires of the person we will be at that future point in time. Yet, our imaginations are limited in projecting our future selves. It is impossible to predict who we will be in the future. If we waste time thinking about how our futures are supposed to be, we miss out on our actual lives. That is, all of our attention is focused on worry and fear of not getting what we *think* we want in the future.

We can easily become attached to these mental images and then struggle with ourselves to make them come true. When we cling to an image of what are lives need to be we lose sight of all other possibilities. If you have fantasized about being with a man who is six-foot-two and then you meet a man who is five-foot-nine, will you disregard all the other variables that make him a perfect match for you because he is shorter than you dreamed he would be? Or will you allow yourself to be happy?

We don't just project ourselves into the future. We also do it to the people in our lives, especially our partners and children. We can easily become preoccupied idealizing who we want them to be in the future. If you project a future for a loved one, you are doing yourself and your loved one a huge a disservice. Not to mention wasting a considerable amount of energy trying to reconcile your mental image with reality.

If your partner works for you today, then let him work for you today. If he makes you happy now, don't let what is going on in your head cause you to be unhappy with him artificially. You are making assumptions about who this person will be and who you will be in the future. But you have no clue who you, or he will be; the future is only a fabrication of your imagination. It is a lot easier to deal with yourself and people in the here and now.

All the drama that ensues from the creation of the future self and the fear of not achieving the ideal life can cause unnecessary stress. Our fight for happiness in the future causes us to sacrifice our happiness today. We often become preoccupied with a future that doesn't exist and might not ever come to pass, driven by the desires of today and the plan for tomorrow. But we shouldn't prioritize tomorrow's happiness over today's happiness.

Maximize your happiness today because that is all you are guaranteed. One way to accomplish this is to disregard the projected images of your future. Leave the door open to be whoever you are going to be when that time arrives.

Too often we are absent from living our lives. We don't appreciate the great experiences and people who surround us each and every day because we are fantasizing about the future. For instance, we hit a milestone age and instead of celebrating that we got to live another year we get upset and complain because we think we aren't living the life we think we should be living. We are afraid we are missing out on something. We fear time is running out. The truth is that we are just distracting ourselves from experiencing: fulfillment, joy, and happiness in the here and now. The only life we should be concerned with is the current life.

Live each day as it unfolds because life is ephemeral. You get to choose how you want to spend each day of your life. Do you want to spend it worrying? Or would you rather be able to look back on your life and say that you lived your best life with no fear or reservations? It is your choice.

Something that happens when we envision our future selves is that we become concerned about growing old alone. There is a real psychology behind this fear. It is the fear that we alone aren't enough and therefore can't survive on our own. People go to extreme measures to avoid growing old alone, including staying in bad relationships, marrying people they don't love, or settling for undesirable partners. As people, we want to be surrounded by those who love and care about us. It bothers us to think about a future that is lonely with no one to love and care for us. But if we are fortunate enough to live that long, we are projecting ourselves 30–40 years in the future. It isn't so unreasonable to envision what your life may look like two or three years from now, but starts to get more unreasonable to project that far into the future.

Who knows what is going to happen between now and then? Life is so unpredictable. Frankly, you might not even live that long. Do you really need to worry about how you are going to feel or where you are going to be when you are 70 or 80 years old? That is too far in the future to worry about now. Everything is subject to change. It stands to reason that your life will be completely different ten years from now, let alone decades from now. Why suffer now from fears of being lonely in the future when it isn't your reality at the present moment?

The creation and projection of the future self is limiting.

Have you ever feared growing old alone? *That is a self-imposed limitation.*

Do you feel it is too late to meet the love of your life? *That is a self-imposed limitation.*

Have you ever thought time is running out for you to achieve your dreams? *That is a self-imposed limitation.* There is no defined period of time written into law that dictates when we are supposed to achieve certain things, if at all.

Self-imposed limitations are the confines we create in our minds that give us a sense of security and comfort. It is often said that the mind that perceives limitation is the limitation. We tend to stretch to what we perceive as our maximum. But most of us only stretch to the maximum of our comfort zone. We construct mental limitations all the time about who we think we are, what we think we need, and what we should or shouldn't do. And then we confine ourselves to these self-imposed limitations because we don't realize there is more space beyond the walls we have built in our mind.

It isn't wrong for us to have intentions for the future and envision what that might entail. It does however become unjustifiable to become so attached to those preconceived notions that we see no other possibility. There are ways we can have a dream for the future without becoming stuck in the dream. We can hold an intention to create a certain future, but should give ourselves the space not to be bound by it.

You can become so attached to the dream for a certain outcome that you end up narrowly locking yourself into one option rather than giving yourself the opportunity to explore all the other alternatives. Instead you can choose to view the future as a mystery, full of excitement. You don't know what is going to happen, but you are excited about its unfolding. If you live your life fully now you won't have to worry about the future.

CHAPTER 10
Surrendering

*Our lives are nothing but collective experiences. If our lives
are the summation of individual experiences and we create
blockages with perceived problems, or are absent witnesses,
then we miss those experiences, and therefore miss life.*

THERE ARE THINGS that are in our control, but there are
far more things that are out of our control. It is important to
understand this, because too often we are consumed with controlling our lives.

As an example, do you believe you are in control of the
people you meet in your life? Think about the people you know:
family, friends, classmates, and coworkers. You weren't in control of meeting any of these people. You were born into your
family and had no say. You randomly met your friends by being
engaged in a life experience. So why is it that we believe it is up
to us to meet the loves of our lives? When it doesn't happen in
our defined timeline, why do we blame ourselves?

Think about how truly enchanting that idea is: One day
you are in the right place at the right time and meet a person who touches your soul so deeply that the two of you are

willing to surrender yourselves to one another to experience life together. Do you really believe you are capable of that level of orchestration and coordination?

That which you can't control is that which you shouldn't agonize over. This doesn't mean you sit back and expect miracles to happen for the things you want. You still make an effort to accomplish the things you want in life. But when you understand that you aren't in control, you relinquish blame and embrace that your life is exactly as intended.

There are those who think they are in the driver's seat of their lives and as a result force themselves into less desirable situations. They are forcing answers on themselves in order to resolve problems that aren't really problems, when they should instead surrender to their life journey.

Some people mistakenly think of surrender negatively. Surrender doesn't mean giving up or not caring. It doesn't mean having no personal agency to achieve the things you want to accomplish in life. Or being a victim of fate. Surrendering is allowing yourself to let go of your self-imposed limitations in order to move beyond your mental boundaries and allow yourself to embrace and accept possibility.

Our lives are nothing but collective experiences. If our lives are the summation of individual experiences and we create blockages with perceived problems, or are absent witnesses, then we miss those experiences, and therefore miss life.

One of the first steps to surrendering is acknowledging that you are ultimately not in control of your journey. You can set intentions. You can choose from the options that are presented to you. You can state your preferences. But you have to accept that these things are out of your control.

I think you can agree with this. The proof this is true is in your own life. Even if things are going according to plan, one day you lose your job, develop an unforeseen illness, get into a car accident, or a loved one dies. Or if things aren't going so well you suddenly find out that you are getting a raise or you won the lottery—or you could turn a corner in the street and crash right into the love of your life. The point is we can't know what tomorrow will bring, so we must surrender our expectations of control to the unknown.

Life is so unpredictable. As soon as we start to think we have it all figured out, life has a way of proving us wrong. Once you accept that there is much to life that is out of your control, then you can begin to embrace life and start allowing events to occur as intended instead of worrying about what could happen. If you pay attention you will notice that most of the time we worry about situations that never even occur.

Once you surrender, you begin to realize a few things. You realize that the past is prologue. You appreciate that you are exactly where you need to be. You discover that much of your drama and self-inflicted suffering is a figment of your imagination. You recognize that the future doesn't yet exist and will turn out exactly how it is supposed to be.

Not surrendering to your life journey is like trying to cheat death.

There are those who fear dying and take needless precautions to maintain and extend their lives. They are so afraid to live that they are limiting their experience in a meaningless way.

Say that you fear death and lock yourself in your house. You believe if you leave the house your chance of dying is more likely. You never get on a plane to go on vacation and explore the world because you are scared the plane might crash. You deprive yourself of savoring rich and tasty foods, and instead only eat lettuce, because you believe other foods are unhealthy and cause disease. You are consumed with worry and think of ways you can avoid risk at any cost. Thus, you live a half life.

You do all of these things and then one day, while locked in your house, having never traveled anywhere, and eating only lettuce, you get out of bed and suddenly have a massive heart attack and die. How would you feel having lived like that? Disappointed, right? Tragedies like this are happening all around us every day. Just pick up a newspaper or turn on the news and you will hear all kinds of tragic stories about people dying from sickness, murder, natural disasters, plane crashes, terrorism, or other unforeseen events. Do you think these people expected that they were going to die? No. But they did.

The same is true if you try to predict and control every aspect of your life. You are taking measured steps in order to have your life look a certain way. In the end, there are going to be things that happen that are far out of your control that will alter your life forever. So, surrender and stop trying to control every outcome and prevent everything bad from happening. Don't be so afraid that you aren't going to get what you want out of life that you start limiting your own experience. You can't cheat death, but you can certainly cheat life.

The second aspect of surrendering is embracing your individuality and realizing that your path in life is unique. We have to stop the bad habit of comparing ourselves to everyone. We think, "*She owns a nicer house than mine.*""*She makes more money than me.*""*Her husband is more successful than mine.*""*She has the perfect family and I don't." "She is prettier than me."*

No one has the same story as you. No one has the same path as you. There is only one you. There will only ever be one you. The truth in that is truly remarkable. Do yourself a favor and represent yourself well. If you are busy trying to be someone else, then how can you fulfill your purpose? Stop trying to make your life look like everyone else's. It is yours and yours alone, so let it be distinct. When you really understand this concept, you will see that your life is unfolding as intended. You realize that you are exactly where you need to be and that there was a series of events that led you to this very moment. You will start to view your life very differently because you will accept life as it is.

We spend an inordinate amount of time and money allowing others to tell us what we should believe and who we should be. Don't get caught in the trap of thinking that you need to strive to be anything more than your true self. The best example of this is relationship advice books. Don't be misguided into thinking that all of these books are here to serve you. Often, their authors are interested in capitalizing on your weakness. If we were to take the advice of some of these "experts," they would have us change the very fabric of our being.

Temporarily altering our actions doesn't change who we are. We may go through life attempting to change who we are to achieve a goal. We tip-toe around ourselves so much that we can no longer hear ourselves. We lose ourselves, and don't even know who we truly are. We make minor tweaks here and there, hoping they will yield different results, but we are really just doing patchwork. We aren't addressing any of our real issues, which would require a more massive undertaking. You will end up spending a lot of time and energy altering who you are out of fear of not being who you think you need to be.

More importantly, do we really need to change who we are? There are things about each of us that we need to work on to better ourselves, but should we change ourselves as a means to an end? The truth is we aren't really changing ourselves from within. We are just taking measured steps to temporarily change ourselves on the surface to become appealing.

You aren't being true to yourself if you pretend to be someone different. You are just pretending to be someone that you aren't in order to achieve an ideal. This is why we often hear people complain about how their spouses changed after marriage. In fact, their partner didn't change. They were always like that and decided to finally give up the charade. They no longer feel the need to expend the energy to be someone different to obtain their partners' affections.

We don't need to part with our true nature for the sake of attaining a goal. We can work on getting to know ourselves better, identify the parts of us that require work, and then be the best us. There is no need to be someone we aren't, or discard who we are just to check the box. In *The Wisdom of No Escape*, Pema Chodron wisely says, "Our brilliance, our juiciness, our spiciness, is all mixed up with our craziness and our confusion, and therefore it doesn't do any good to try and get rid of our so-called negative aspects, because in that process we also get rid of our basic wonderfulness."[1] Rather than getting rid of the parts of us that we label as bad, we should gain familiarity with those parts of us to strengthen our being.

We all desire to embrace our individuality and live life according to our own rules. We all desire and deserve to be happy. That is, after all, what we truly are searching for. We simply want to be happy.

Everyone talks about happiness. But what is it to truly be happy? We are constantly told we should be happy, which doesn't give us permission to be anything other than that. Intellectually we understand that we should be happy. Yet it is a challenge to be happy. So then, what is it to truly be happy?

Here's something simple I learned about happiness. If you want to be happy, then you have to give yourself the permission to feel sad. It took me a long time to figure out that I didn't have to kick myself every time I was having a bad day. In my head, I believed I was this spiritually evolved being who had it all figured out and wasn't supposed to feel anything other than happy. I ended up feeling guilty about having a bad day, which put me one level lower than the feeling of my sadness. There will certainly be days when you are sad, no matter how evolved you think you are. Sadness is as much a human emotion as happiness.

From what I can tell, life isn't about feeling blissfully happy all day, every day. It is about the journey. Our evolution. In order to evolve, we must experience all the facets of our multi-faceted feelings. It is part of the human experience.

All happiness means is to be at peace with yourself, even when you are sad. All it takes is surrendering to your life's journey and being satisfied and content with who and where you are in your life. Happiness isn't about judging yourself, someone else, or life for not giving you the things that you think you ought to have.

As people, we put so many conditions on our happiness. We are constantly waiting for our lives to start. It is the

"I can only be happy if" syndrome. "*I can only be happy if I'm married.*" "*I can only be happy if I make a certain amount of money.*" "*I can only be happy if I live in a certain zip code.*" "*I can only be happy if someone else loves me.*" We are so busy trying to remedy all of these conditions that we don't achieve our single biggest desire: *happiness*.

It is said there is no end to desire. It is true. As soon as we get one thing we begin pining for the next, and the next and the next. It is part of the human condition. Stop waiting to attain all your desires before you can start to allow yourself to be happy. It is almost impossible because we will inevitably always want more. Stop holding your breath waiting for your life to start, waiting to be happy, thinking, "*I thought I would be happy by now.*" That is absolutely of no service to you.

There is more than one road. There is no need to walk the same road as everyone else. In fact, there are no roads if you choose to fly. *So fly!*

You don't have to be like everyone else. Your life doesn't need to look like what you have been taught is a perfect life; you just think it does in order to be happy. Happiness is a choice. You don't need anyone or anything to be happy. You can simply choose to be happy.

You may have convinced yourself that there is only one road to happiness, that if you follow the defined life plan you will be guaranteed happiness. There is no formula for happiness. Once you accept that, you will free yourself from the concept that anything external to ourselves is a prerequisite for happiness.

You can attain joy through any life you chose to lead. Once you understand this, you will stop searching and searching. Your desire to conform to society's expectations to achieve the perfect, happy life is nothing but a figment of your imagination. Your happiness is a conscious choice. You can choose to be happy despite your circumstance. Or you can choose not to be. All that needs to occur is that you choose to think beyond a limited idea of how you achieve happiness.

CONCLUSION
The Future of Now

Human evolution is driven by human choice.

WE ARE AT a cultural turning point. The tides are rising and a storm is brewing on the horizon. All it takes is our willingness to be open to change and not get stuck in the past. The change I speak of is the cultural shift in the thinking about what it is to be a woman. In the coming years, we are going to see the feminine identity, as we currently understand it, redefined due to a number of factors, which include the following.

- The growing number of women in higher education
- Women continuing to assume larger roles in society
- Urbanization, creating an interchangeable marketplace
- Our affinity for a knowledge-based information economy
- New family structures emerging
- A blending of beliefs and traditions resulting from interracial and cross-cultural coupling

As women and men continue to redefine their gender roles, continuing the progression of social change that began in the last century, we are going to see a shedding of the past ideals surrounding the feminine identity.

In the past, we were handed an archetype and told that we needed to survive within its constraints, never thinking we had the authority to question or challenge the system. It was a system that was reflective of the beliefs of archaic times where women were considered less than whole. We have since become empowered to challenge the commonly held perceptions about who we need to be. We live in new era where we are confident, educated, and ambitious.

A new paradigm for what it means to be a woman is currently burning in the hearts and minds of women. We question stepping beyond these boundaries because of what we have been taught. Instead, we question ourselves if we don't fit the ideal of what is acceptable. In time, women will forgo the idea that there is only one destiny and path to happiness.

In the future, a much broader continuum will exist of what defines a successful woman's life. New expectations are emerging as we redefine our identities. The boundaries of what it is to have a meaningful life have expanded. We want purpose. We want to feel fulfilled. We want to be seen as individuals. We don't want to be reduced to a one-size-fits-all path that limits our options. We want access to multiple paths that lead us to holistic living. We want to exercise our free will to make the best decisions for our lives and not out of expectation. We are able to live our best lives when we are able to clearly set intentions for ourselves.

What is key is that we don't have to give up our desire for partnering and having children, if we so chose, in the process of defining a self. Partnering and procreating is very much who we are. It is part of the human experience. Sharing our love only helps to serve our spiritual evolution. Bringing life into this world is a gift that should be treasured. To deny something so seemingly beautiful is to deny creation. All that needs to happen is we let go of our attachment to the idea that life needs to be a certain way; let go of the belief of who we think we need to be; let go of the fear of not getting what we want out of life.

We have a habit of basing the future on the past because we know it so well. We fear what we don't understand. The way for change, therefore, is to believe in the possibilities of the unknown. Believe in a new day. That is how revolutionary thinkers pave the way. They aren't complacent, thinking life should exist as is; rather they have the foresight to believe in endless possibilities.

Social change is nothing but a shift in our mindset and thinking. This change can and will be possible if you make it your own personal reality. We are a people of change and have the power to make such change happen. I don't know what the future holds, but I do know what the future can look like if we rethink our deeply held beliefs, carefully crafting our own paths, and define how we would like to live our lives.

We hold many rigid, compromising beliefs about who we need to be and how we should be living our lives. Wear your beliefs lightly. The belief that your life needs to be a certain way is the biggest misconception you hold. Your life is evolving into something new every day. If you allow yourself to accept the system of your misguided beliefs then you are preventing yourself from growing. In order to consciously grow your own way, you have to investigate who you are and what you believe.

Human evolution is driven by human choice. If you truly believe this type of change isn't possible, then it won't be, but only for you, because you have defined your personal reality to be that way.

We don't have to wait for change to be popularized to feel comfortable or bold enough to start embracing our individuality and living our truth. We can be the change we want to see right now.

Maybe you don't want to see change because you like how things are. That is fine as long as it is a personal decision you have made for yourself, and not based on what you are told is the only acceptable way of life. You should live life according to your own dictates.

If you are like me, then you believe change is warranted. However, if we continue to go down the path to seek a new model, it isn't about replacing one model for the next. We don't have to all be on the same side of the equation. Our definitions of womanhood don't need to be identical. Rather, it is about opening the door to new perspectives that work for each individual. We can choose to define the stories of our lives for ourselves. The future is ours right now. We don't need to wait. We can individually live these truths for ourselves now.

NOTES

Chapter 1   Changing Expectations
   1. Betty Friedan, *The Feminine Mystique* (New York: W.W. Norton, 1963).

Chapter 2   Love
   1. M. Scott Peck, *The Road Less Traveled (Timeless Edition): A New Psychology of Love, Traditional Values and Spiritual Growth* (New York: Touchstone, 2003): p. 89.

Chapter 3   The Evolution of Her
   1. Stephanie Coontz, *Marriage, a History: How Love Conquered Marriage* (New York: Penguin Group, 2005).

Chapter 4   Rituals & Traditions
   1. R. & L. Brasch, *How Did It Begin: The Origins of Our Curious Customs and Superstitions* (New York: Fine Communications, 2006): p. 71.
   2. Laurence Cawley, "Do People Spend a Month's Salary on an Engagement Ring?" *BBC News Magazine* (May 16, 2014).
   3. Caroline Myss, *Anatomy of the Spirit: The Seven Stages of Power and Healing* (New York: Three Rivers Press, 1996).

Chapter 9   Projecting into the Future
   1. Jordi Quoidbach, Daniel T. Gilbert, and Timothy D. Wilson, "The End of History Illusion" *Science Magazine* (January 2013).

Chapter 10   Surrendering
   1. Pema Chodron, *The Wisdom of No Escape: And the Path of Loving Kindness* (Boston, MA.: Shambhala, 2001): p. 46.

ABOUT THE AUTHOR

HEATHER STANISLAUS embarked on a journey of self-discovery over ten years ago through the practice of yoga and meditation. She is a thought-provoking, contemporary woman dedicated to guiding individuals to apply wisdom in their every-day lives and uncover their personal truth.

www.ingramcontent.com/pod-product-compliance
Lightning Source LLC
Chambersburg PA
CBHW022338280326
41934CB00006B/689